Dr. Beechick's
HOMESCHOOL
Answer Book

W9-ADD-493

ISBN 0-940319-12-8

90000>

9 780940 319127

Dr. Beechick's
HOMESCHOOL
Answer Book

Ruth Beechick

Selected and Edited
by
Debbie Strayer

arrow press

Arrow Press
Pollock Pines CA 95726
Distributor:
8825 Blue Mountain Dr.
Golden Co 80403

Library of Congress Catalog Card Number: 98-71003

Cover art by: MDC Publishing Services, Brunswick, Ohio.

© 1998 by Arrow Press.

Printed in Canada.

ISBN 0-940319-12-8

Contents

Ruth's Introduction

On the phone one day Debbie said, "You should make a book out of your questions and answers."

I responded, "That idea crosses my mind every once in a while but I push it down, because I have too many other priorities ahead of it."

"How about if I do it?"

"Good idea. Go ahead and do it, if you want."

That's the conversation reconstructed as best I remember it, and this book has moved forward rapidly since then.

My association with Debbie goes back a number of years. She was the first editor of "Homeschooling Today," and built that magazine's reputation for high quality. I was proud to be a columnist in her magazine, answering questions that readers sent in. Besides the magazine, we appeared together at homeschool conferences in question-and-answer sessions.

So over the years we have collected numerous questions. We know which questions are asked most often, which questions trouble homeschoolers deeply, and the wide range in between. Many questions included here are reprints from the magazine, and others came from conferences. In cases where we have tapes of the conference sessions, I have taken the liberty of rewriting my answers. The beauty of being a writer rather than a speaker is that I can change my words the next day, and I like to do that. Debbie has selected and arranged everything into the book form you now hold.

I admire all you brave and hard-working homeschool parents. I appreciate what you are doing for our society by building your strong families. And I will be gratified if any thoughts and ideas in this book are of help to you. Debbie and I both commit this work to the Lord and pray that He will use it in this wonderful movement of homeschooling.

Debbie's Introduction

You're going crazy. You've tried everything you know to do. Still your homeschooling problem has not been resolved. You've asked friends, support group members and read whatever books you could get your hands on. What is left to do?

If you've been blessed as I have, the answer comes quickly—ask Ruth. When I've come to the end of my resources (and my wits) this thought has lifted my spirits like an answered prayer. I'll call Ruth and ask her, and she has always graciously helped, guided and encouraged.

What she offers is a wealth of knowledge and experience and an even rarer commodity—wisdom. She listens with a caring ear and offers practical, sensible advice. She never hesitates to direct me to another author or resource if it's needed, and in the answering, I always come away with something more precious than a solution to a math or reading problem. Invariably, what I come away with is peace.

It is my prayer that this book will be like that phone call for you. I hope the question you have is answered here, or the direction you need is revealed. But most of all, I pray that the gift of encouragement and wisdom minister to you as you read, and that you too can share in the fruit of Ruth's deep and abiding trust in God—His peace and His provision.

1. Philosophy and Learning Theory

Who Do You Ask When You're the Teacher?

Ruth's Answers to Questions on Education Theory

I have been a teacher since 1977 when I finished my master's degree in special education, and a homeschooler since 1988 when my son became a kindergartner. You would think that with all these experiences I would have a calm, cool and collected response for every question of an educational nature. The truth is that often I can come up with an answer in educational jargon; one that sounds good but may not mean a lot. I answer questions in this way when people are antagonistic about homeschooling, or are educators themselves. They seem to expect answers in this teacher-speak.

This section of questions and answers is not like that. Ruth answers questions about education theory by identifying the real issue for homeschoolers and then pointing them towards a commonsense answer. But don't mistake her answers for not being educationally sound. They certainly are that; they are just written in such a way that anyone can understand them. So thank you Ruth, for helping us demystify teaching and learning.

By the way—now that my children are older, I find that they can give the best answers to people's questions about homeschooling. Not only does it reassure the questioner about my children's abilities, it also enables them to hear homeschooling described on a first-hand level. Having listened to my answers and my husband's to questions about homeschooling for the past ten years, our children are more than able spokespeople. After all, to them, it's just the way we live.

—Debbie

Q. *Please help me understand the different types of educational philosophies I hear about at homeschool conventions. Do I need to formulate my own philosophy of education as the speakers tell me to?*

A. One reason there is so much confusion is that we use the word philosophy on two different levels. Used technically in education, it refers to underlying beliefs of truth and knowledge upon which we base decisions about what children should learn. Used in its everyday sense, it can mean almost anything. People can take a "philosophical attitude," being calm in the face of trouble. Or they say their philosophy on raising children is to be strict with them.

To further confuse the picture, the term is often interchanged with educational psychology, which refers to the underlying psychological views upon which we base decisions about how to teach children—the methods and the best ages and such. Philosophy helps us decide *what* to teach, and psychology helps us decide *how* to teach it.

I see no reason why homeschoolers should study the various educational philosophies to determine where they fit in, and especially not before they begin teaching. I can tell you ahead of time, if you're a Christian, that you won't fit into any of the philosophies they teach in a standard course. They'll say that you're "eclectic," that you draw a little from each of the philosophies. But they've got it backward. You're the one who has the correct and whole view of truth and knowledge, and each of the philosophies draws a little from that view.

It's really quite simple to just say that you have a Christian philosophy of education. When you're shopping for curriculum, you'll want to put the Bible itself in your plans. And all the other subjects you want from a Biblical perspective. This Biblical perspective is more important in subjects like literature and history than in a subject like arithmetic, but you'll know that without me telling you.

After you have homeschooled for a year or two is a better time to try writing the kind of essay that some of the speakers mean. By this time you can better express some meaningful thoughts about your Christian philosophy of education. Tell how it affects your choice of long-range goals (yes, mention goals), and some of the ways you plan to reach the goals. These latter points are your methods, of course, but you can mix it all up on your essay. Just write a plain language, down-home statement of what you want to accomplish in your homeschooling, and how you'll go about doing it.

Q. What is the Charlotte Mason approach and what do you think of it? What about Raymond and Dorothy Moore's position that later is better than early for formal instruction? It is very confusing out there. Sometimes just buying a textbook and workbook seems to be the easiest answer to the curriculum questions I have!

A. Charlotte Mason had some good ideas for teaching children. If you like them you can try them anytime; it doesn't take special curriculum to do it. As I read her, she was writing to tell parents what they could do at home with their children, who were not strictly homeschoolers but who were also attending English schools of her time. Thus the ideas tend to be the more natural ones of enjoying stories, observing nature and such. The more systematic, structured teaching was left to the schools.

Raymond Moore's writings on beginning reading come from a good knowledge of the pertinent research. He is highly competent to evaluate the research, and one of the most experienced in modern times. Homeschoolers would do well to listen to him. I agree with him and Dorothy on this and on almost everything they write about homeschooling.

"Later is better" has come to be a slogan, and it sometimes is misused. I'd say that if you have a choice of starting too early or starting too late, it's better to start too late, since you won't damage eye development or something. But, actually, you don't have to make that kind of choice, and Dr. Moore's book doesn't say that. It mainly points out the dangers of starting too early. Your real problem is to find the optimum time for your individual child.

These writers, and others, can inform you on numerous aspects of teaching, and they can stimulate your thinking. But don't read with the idea that you have to get teaching all figured out before you know what books to buy. That's impossible. Your idea of just buying a book is okay while you still feel confused.

If you're just beginning, you may choose something more structured than you'll want the second year, so don't buy very much at first. You can use the books in many ways: you read or the child reads, a big chunk or a small chunk, and so on. But if you just can't make it fit at all, you won't be the first homeschooler to discard the early purchases and try again. I could add that even in the classroom some of this juggling goes on, especially at the beginning of a school year when the teacher is learning to know the pupils.

Q. The classical approach is very popular right

*now. What is the classical approach? I see this
advertised, and I wonder if it's as good as it sounds.
Do you think all homeschoolers should adopt it?*

A. Historically speaking, classical education is
Hellenistic education, which of course was
pagan. During Roman times, Latin language
and literature were added to the Greek form,
and Christians then had various ways of
Christianizing that Latin classical education.
Christian leaders of the time debated whether
they should do this or whether they should
instead formulate a separate, fully Christian
education. The Jews were doing so. But the
Christians never managed to make the separation.

Now, interestingly, in the homeschool
movement we seem to be in the same situation
as those early Christians. We want a Christian
education and we are casting about for the best
way to do this. Most of the classical curriculums
being offered to homeschoolers have Christian
teaching added in one way or another.

The Catholics have long used their version
of classical education in both Europe and
America. Mortimer Adler with his long and
brilliant education career and his Great Books
program, has done a lot for classical education
in our times. Today you will find homeschool
writers describing their various versions of
classical education. But most include study of
the ancient Greek and Latin languages and their
classic authors, along with the logic and thinking involved in debating the ideas of those
authors. (Here's where the Christians say to

compare the ideas with Bible teachings.) In addition, these curriculum writers have certain beliefs about what children should learn at various ages, such as memorizing and facts first; then logic and thinking about those facts. This gets into the psychological aspects of learning, and I can't take space here to discuss those issues.

But for people like you who are wondering what to do with classical education, I would like to suggest putting the Bible first. This is the greatest of all the great books. With Bible education as the core, you can add on any classical education that you like. Compare classical authors with Paul and other Bible writers, in a reverse of what happens if you have a core classical curriculum and add on the Bible. Every bit as much logic and thinking can happen this way. In higher education during the Middle Ages, theology was called the Queen of the Sciences; everything else was to flow from that. Maybe that's an ancient ideal to revive.

Actually, I think some of you homeschoolers are heading in that direction. Instinctively, you know that the Bible should have pre-eminence. Wouldn't it be exciting if modern homeschoolers achieve what the early Christians failed to achieve in education—not a Christianized pagan curriculum, but an education fully Christian at its core?

Note: If Debbie and I had had more Latin we probably would use the Latin plural form curricula, *but we have chosen to use the more common English form* curriculums *in this book.*

Q. My husband and I are homeschooling our daughter (10) and son (9), and have another son (5) and daughter (1). We concentrate on the basics of reading, writing, and arithmetic and use unit studies.

What suggestions do you have for adapting the classical model of education for homeschool use? At what age should Latin be started and how should it be taught? Also, when and how does one teach thinking skills in the classical model?

A. When I think of a classical education, I think of its broader use as promoted by Mortimer Adler and other great educators and as practiced in a few colleges and now in some elementary and high schools. I do not equate it with any particular publisher or advertiser in the homeschool movement. In a nutshell, this means to educate children in great classics, particularly of our Western civilization. (See the preceding answer for further description.) Those classics have shaped philosophy and thinking and life down to our times. Thinking is so built into this education that you can't avoid it. When you read and try to understand the classics you'll be thinking about the great themes that have occupied the minds of men in the past.

Young children often begin with Aesop's fables, and, of course, Bible stories. The Bible, the greatest classic of all, should be studied thoroughly and be the measure by which we Christians evaluate all the others. Your older children could read Aesop's fables to the 5-year-old and see if he can figure out the moral usually given in the final sentence. Plenty of thinking will happen while they try to explain the meanings. Write in your record book that they are discussing analogies, if you want to make it sound impressive. Analogies are often included in standardized tests for measuring thinking ability.

After Aesop you can use children's versions of heroic ancient stories and, again, of Bible stories. Since many classics are advanced or college level, you can try using selected portions that introduce your children to certain writers or to themes that you want them to know about. Writers like Augustine, Luther and Calvin should feature in teaching our Christian heritage. Studying such writers will involve logic and thinking at every level.

As for Latin, I'd say to wait until the children read and write well in English, maybe about sixth grade, or before that if you like. Believers in classical education start early on Latin, but I suggest that since Latin is a dead language, there is not the same need as with modern languages for working on pronunciation at young ages. So a later start can still work well. For home study you could use any books or tapes or software that seem workable to you. It probably would help to have more than one item so if you get bogged down with one book you can switch to something else for a while. In a catalog I saw *Winnie the Pooh* in Latin. I suppose the "classical people" would not include that, but it sounds like fun to me.

Q. How do you motivate a reluctant learner, an 11-year-old boy? He thinks everything is boring even before we start. His retention is low because of his lack of interest.

A. Motivation is a big topic in education circles, and a controversial one. The pro side says that a teacher needs a bag of tricks to motivate for this lesson and that. The con side says that children have an innate desire to learn, and if we don't turn it off, and if the lessons are within the child's ability, and so forth, we don't need to work at motivating.

I lean more toward the con side, but I'd use whatever I needed on the pro side, also. That is, when necessary I would work at stimulating interest. I would reward and praise.

But all the while, I would be trying to figure out what is wrong. Why isn't the child showing a natural curiosity and interest in at least some of the studies? Quite often the real problem is not lack of motivation, but the child uses that to cover up some inability. It saves face to say that he doesn't want to do something rather than to say that he can't do it. I'd be trying to decide if the work is beyond the ability of the child or if he can't understand it or can't read it or whatever. What about physical problems, nutrition, energy level?

In cases of neurological problems, such as that the eyes don't focus well and tire easily, children don't even know they have an eye problem. They don't know what a normal condition is; they only know how it is for them.

In schools sometimes the problem is peer pressure, where a child feels he has to act uninterested in order to be accepted by his

14

peers. I suppose that problem can creep into homeschooling in some situations, but time and separation from such peers should solve it.

While you're trying to solve the underlying problem, it's okay to simply require work you think your son should do. As his skills improve and as his mind gets involved in various tasks, he will begin to find that some studies are interesting. That develops "intrinsic motivation," and it's the real kind, better than the "extrinsic motivation" found in teachers' bags of tricks.

Q. My son, who is now 14, should begin ninth grade soon. We have been homeschooling for five years, since fourth grade.

My son is intelligent and enjoys learning. His favorite subjects are Bible and history. He performs well in all subjects when he's in the mood. But presently we are suffering from burnout. We both need a break. Perhaps a long one—like a sabbatical.

We've been schooling in three-week spurts with a week or two between sessions in hopes that the breaks would help. Also, we do home maintenance projects and other activities for variety, but I am finding it almost impossible to get him to settle down to study for decent lengths of time, or to discipline himself to any kind of schedule.

He pokes through his lessons unless there is a special incentive. He doesn't like to be nagged, but seldom produces work on his own initiative. He despises writing anything. In my opinion, he should be developing independent study skills with ready guidance when necessary.

Help! I am very frustrated.

A. Your letter arrived in February, and I call February and March the burnout months of the school year. But your problem sounds more than seasonal, so I'll suggest some other thoughts to pursue.

First, in such situations, I think parents need to determine whether there is a heart problem. These have spiritual solutions, and they must be solved before you can make much progress on the learning. If your son is cheerful and cooperating with other family activities, then this probably is not the case here.

Next, remember that young teenagers have their problems of dealing with physical changes and growth spurts both in their bodies and their brains. I think homeschoolers miss much of the emotional turmoil of these years by spending less time with peers. But you can't miss all the physical and mental turmoil.

Growth spurt in the brain doesn't mean the students suddenly learn more and study more. It means, instead, that they need time to assimilate the new growth. Think of a boy suddenly growing tall; he needs time to become comfortable with his new height and to manage his long legs gracefully and so forth. Then apply that same principle to brain growth.

So it would be okay to back off on some studies. For instance, require only a minimum of writing for a while. In math, it wouldn't hurt to delay algebra for a year. Let him concentrate on his first loves of Bible and history. Over the highschool years you can balance things out according to his career goals; it doesn't all have to be balanced now in ninth grade.

The opposite possibility to consider is that the junior high materials you are using might not be challenging enough for your son. Textbooks for these years contain much repetition of material from sixth grade and earlier. Some homeschoolers are learning to skip these books with good students and move directly into highschool level work.

As for developing independent study habits, you'll have to break this down into much smaller goals. For instance, invent a simple system in which the boy himself records the work he completes each day. Give him the incentive of free time or something after he finishes your essential schoolwork requirements and records his work. Later, extend this daily requirement to a week. Within the week he could plan his own time, such as doing the hated writing assignment on Monday or letting it slide until Friday. With consistent structure from you, along with praise and encouragement, he should gradually gain skill in planning his time. When I taught college, I would have been glad for more students who had learned what I consider essential work habits.

After having said all this on structure and traditional teaching style, I should add that as a homeschooler you can elect an entirely different route. What about an apprenticeship, working part time with a willing master? What about taking a month to get an old motorcycle into running condition? Or go ahead and take that sabbatical. What would your son do with a sabbatical? In the real world sabbaticals are not do-nothing vacations; they are renewals by means of a change of pace, and people set goals to reach during their sabbaticals.

The job of teaching often consists of solving tough problems such as you present here. You're on the right track by trying various approaches. Keep trying until something works and your son comes successfully through these young teen years.

Q. I am concerned about pushing my two boys too hard and giving them too much too soon. They seem to enjoy the breadth and depth I teach, but am I setting them up for burnout?

A. If your boys enjoy their studies, you are setting them up for a life of discipline and hard work, rather than for burnout. Burnout comes not from work that is mentally engrossing, as yours seems to be, but from unsuitable work, either too much mindless busywork or too much pushing beyond the boys' present ability.

But remember to lighten up once in a while with a change of pace—something like a day trip or a Friday of free time.

Q. How can I tell when I need to give my 8-year-old son an extra push with his school work and when I just need to wait for more maturity on his part?

A. I don't know any easy trick or formula to use for this purpose. Try a variety of tactics. For one, don't push at all in reading. At age 8 he is probably in the fluency building stage of reading and should read a lot of easy material. So let him enjoy easy books, and forget about workbook exercises, comprehension questions and all that. Go easy on spelling, too. Just work occasionally on common, useful words in the context of his writing. Then in arithmetic you could use a more systematic approach, with hard work on lessons in whatever arithmetic program you are using.

As you experiment with these differing amounts of pressure, you can change strategies at any time. For instance, try a month long push on writing good paragraphs, and shorten the arithmetic assignments to compensate. Encourage. Praise. Reward. As your son progresses over the coming months, you should gain a good feel for what he can do and when you should move to the guiding mode instead of the pushing mode.

Q. Is there a different attention span for boys versus girls?

A. I don't take any stock in the information put out on children's attention span. That research usually involves attention to a teacher chosen task. But if the little boy plays with his truck by his own choice, he has an entirely different attention span than the researcher measured, a span usually so long that there seems no need to worry about attention spans at all.

As for comparing boys versus girls on this or any other trait, the figures you read refer only to averages. That is, the average figure from a group of boys may be slightly less than the average of a group of girls, but this tells you nothing about any particular individual in the groups. Many boys in the group would be higher than a lot of the girls.

So statistical averages are not any help when we're working with one particular boy or one particular girl.

Q. My son has the wiggles. What should I do? Should I make him sit still?

A. This is difficult to deal with, especially if you are a relaxed person, and if you have other children studying at the same time as this son, but here are some things to try.

First, plan plenty of physical activity interspersed with short periods of book work. After accomplishing each short book task, your son could run around the house or take out the garbage or climb the stairs or jump rope. Second, just let him wiggle if he seems to concentrate this way, for instance if he can answer questions after listening to you read. Third, as he grows older he should work on sitting still for longer periods. He will need this ability for church and other out-of-home settings. Fourth, look into nutritional matters such as whether sugar bothers him.

Q. People ask me, "Aren't your children missing out socially by not going to school?" I answer that they socialize when it really counts—after school. Are they missing out on something?

A. Your answer probably satisfies most of your questioners. And it's like other answers I hear, where homeschoolers say that their children have church activities and team and club activities and so forth. And I think it's fine to give these answers that your critics understand.

But I can't help wondering if most homeschoolers don't feel they're playing a little game here with the larger society. To meet the question in this fashion is in a sense agreeing with the world that children need many hours of association with their age mates, and saying that homeschoolers provide those hours just as schoolers do. But do we agree? Is it natural to grow up spending many hours per waking day with thirty age-mates? Is this best? Is it Biblical? Or is this just an artificial child life that our part of the world has adopted in fairly recent history?

My opinion is that your children are only missing out on some things you should be happy they miss.

Q. How do I determine what grade level my child is reading at? Is this something we should be concerned with?

A. From the commonsense viewpoint you don't have to be concerned with grade levels. Grades gradually came into being during the 1800s in order to handle increased attendance in the schools. This artificial way of thinking is so entrenched now that we find it difficult to rid ourselves of it. State testing or reporting requirements help keep us tied to grade concepts. But in spite of that, homeschoolers have made great strides in ignoring grade levels, and individualizing instead.

If you do wish or need to know a reading level, it is easy to get a rough estimate simply by having your child read aloud from graded reading textbooks. Textbooks in primary grades usually are numbered to indicate whether they are for the first half of the year or the second half. Begin by reading from a level you think will be easy. If it is, then try the next higher book and so on, until you reach the level where the child misses or struggles with two or three words per page. That level would be considered his instructional level. Above that is frustration level and below that is free reading level.

You can borrow textbooks from many public libraries or from school district professional libraries. These latter are not publicized but are available to you as a taxpayer. Or you may borrow books from your local school. When you obtain a reading level estimate from public school textbooks it should match fairly well with a grade level score on an achievement test. But be aware that books from some major Christian textbook publishers are more difficult. That is, a fifth grade level is published as a fourth grade book, and so on.

Q. How do you not think in terms of grade level when the children have to be tested at grade level? I have to register with my school district at the grade I am teaching.

A. Here you need to think grade levels in connection with the test and registration, but you need not carry it into daily life, such as worrying about the level of each book or science project or grammar rule that you explain. At elementary levels just keep your children reading widely and writing and figuring, and that should be good preparation for the current style of achievement tests.

In some places you may be able to work that grade level situation to your advantage. For instance, if you have a child who is slow in learning to read, you could register him as a second grader instead of a third grader where his age might place him. Then with a second grade test he will score high enough for his grade.

The reverse situation is with an advanced student. If he takes a fourth grade test and scores near the top of the test, you don't know how much higher he could have gone. It would have been better to use a fifth grade test, or even higher. You get the truest score when the child scores near the middle of the range for a particular test. When you're not worried about grade levels, this is not so important that you need to do anything about switching tests. But if you're testing annually and have grade level scores anyway, you might want to think about this.

Here's a story I love about contending with the government's obsession with grade levels. For a time, a particular state ruled that parents could teach their children through seventh grade, but beyond that they had to be certified teachers. So brave, creative parents registered their children as seventh graders until they turned 16 and were no longer required to attend school.

Q. If my son is reading about one grade level lower than his age indicates, how can I enter him into a classroom without him getting—and feeling—way behind?

A. Grade level is a tricky concept. To say "third grade reading level," for instance, is to refer to the level of the average child in third grade. That means half the children in third grade are below that level, and half above. All the political talk of bringing every child up to grade level is nonsense. Any normal classroom has a spread of several grades, and this spread widens as you move higher in the grades. Good teaching widens it even more. To neglect the higher children and work hard to bring up the lower ones may succeed in narrowing the spread, but mostly by depressing the top portion.

So most teachers can handle a child who is below the average of her class in reading. But the school environment tends to intimidate such children and make them feel like failures, while homeschoolers have some of their greatest successes with these children who read later than average.

If you must enter the child in school, you could talk to the teacher who will have him and explain your concerns. Hopefully you will find an understanding teacher who will work with you on this. Also you could talk to your son, explaining that in school some children read better than him and some read like him, but all the children should try to like each other and help each other wherever they can.

If the date of your son's birthday makes him one of the younger children in class, you may wish to put him in the next lower grade. There he could be closer to average in the class. If you think he will always be somewhat lower than the middle, that would be an option to seriously consider. But if you think that once he catches on to reading he can keep up with the older children, then you'd probably not want to do that.

Q. I have a second grader who cries easily and whines a lot in no particular subject. How can I tell if it's a discipline problem or if I'm not reaching her on the right level?

A. You're asking the right question for a situation like this. I might add even a third possibility: perhaps she has some neurological problem such as that her eyes don't focus easily and the effort at book work is too much.

To answer these questions you have to continue your observations. You've already noticed that your daughter whines at any subject, not certain ones. Is it only book work—reading and writing—or is it also projects with clay or math manipulatives? Does she whine at chores? As you gather more clues, you should soon figure out whether it's discipline she needs, or something else.

Q. How can we feel confident about our homeschooling?

A. Confidence builds gradually, I think, as you work hard at homeschooling, solve problems, have some successes and so forth. It is speeded by hearing from others, such as happens in support groups and homeschool writings.

To add my bit, I would say you are in a better position to be a good teacher for your children than I was as a classroom teacher. When you begin teaching one-on-one, mind-to-mind as I like to say it, you very rapidly learn about teaching. I would say that most homeschool moms know more about teaching after a few weeks than I knew after two years of classroom teaching. I was managing a class, trying to keep everybody busy at something profitable hopefully, and only now and then did I have time to work individually with a child who was not getting it or who needed extra challenge or something. I made the greatest strides in understanding children's learning when I worked in summer reading clinics where we solved reading problems with lots of one-on-one work. The fact that you know your children so well and you're dedicated to the job makes you the best teacher your child could have.

I should add that there are also resources to help build your confidence as a homeschooler. One I might recommend is *Gaining Confidence to Teach** by my editor, Debbie Strayer. As a homeschooler herself and a consultant and speaker she really identifies with the struggles homeschoolers face.

*Available from Family Educational Services, 703 Willow Brook Court, Lutz FL 33549. The cost is approximately $14.00.

2.
Curriculum

Choosing Curriculum
That Works
With Your Children

Ten years ago there were very few curriculum choices for homeschoolers. There were one or two publishers who made materials for Christian schools, and that was it. However, with the growth of the homeschooling population has come a wonderful thing—many choices in curriculum, many of them written by homeschoolers themselves. Now you can choose from one book to an entire curriculum, elementary to high school, simple to complex.

One of the blessings of the maturing of the homeschool movement has been this tremendous increase in the amount and kinds of educational materials available to homeschoolers. While I know this is a blessing, I also know that sometimes it can be a mixed blessing. I have seen it on people's faces at curriculum fairs—confusion, uncertainty, even frustration.

Ruth's counsel in this area is valuable, because as always, she directs us not to a particular book, but to finding answers for the underlying problems. I have had the privilege of listening to Ruth talk with those who come up to her at curriculum fairs, seeking her advice. Many times the parent already had an idea of what to do, but felt uncertain without some confirmation. Ruth oftens reaffirms what we know to be true in our hearts, and in this tough area of decision making, we can all use some support.

—*Debbie*

Q. *You say that we Christians should not latch on to any so-called philosophy, but should just say we are Christian educators. That suits me fine, but now I need to know what kind of curriculum I should buy as a Christian educator. It's confusing to see so many claiming to be the Christian approach.*

A. Your philosophy, or your Biblical world-view, guides in choosing what you should teach. So that means teaching the Bible truths themselves and everything else consistent with that. As for how to teach, you are not limited to any particular method or methods.

I know the marketing competition out there sets many people on a search for the best curriculum or the right method. People seem to want to follow a guru, living or dead. They want to fit themselves into a slot with a label. I won't name any slots here; some have long histories and some are newer inventions or adaptations of older ideas. But all, I suggest, are of minor importance in the way you raise your children.

I once wrote a book on Biblical psychology

of learning. There I tried to explain that the center is your child's heart, his discipline and fear of the Lord. Upon that base and within the love of your family, you direct your child's education. That's the most important element.

So lower your expectation of what curriculums will do for you. Don't be a slave to any, even if you primarily follow one. You can use parts, and skip parts. You can switch. You can combine and mix in any order or any proportion.

I hope this view removes some of the stress of shopping and choosing materials to help in your teaching.

Q. Is there a homeschoolers' curriculum that you like? If you were choosing one, what would you use?

A. I can't make specific recommendations for several reasons. One is that I don't have time to evaluate everything. Another is that new materials are constantly appearing, so recommendations in print become outdated.

But I can suggest guidelines. First, I would not load up with one kind of curriculum for everything. It would be deadly to fill in workbooks for every subject, and just as deadly to sit at the computer for every subject.

Second, I would select mainly from materials that have grown out of the home-school movement. These family companies, which sometimes grow quite large, have an advantage over the major education publishers. They know what works in the family setting. They know what they couldn't find to fill their needs, so they wrote it, often for themselves first, and later published it for others. The major companies usually published for classrooms, and when homeschoolers became numerous they began marketing to them, at first without adaptations, and later with adjustments to try to fit the home teaching situation. Large secular publishers have superior marketing skills and they will target homeschoolers more and more in the coming years, but they have major societal obstacles in producing good curriculum. I outline these later in this chapter. Occasionally, for a specialized subject, I might select one of the secular books, but never a full curriculum.

Third, for a good many subjects I would use no curriculum at all, but real books and real life instead. For instance in reading, at least once you're past the decoding stage, there is no point in using a series of graded reading textbooks. I can show ways that these actually slow the progress. Reading real books leads to faster progress, greater vocabulary and knowledge growth, and better preparation for a lifetime of enjoying books. Why have an imitation when you can have the real thing?

Q. What would you consider appropriate as a curriculum for preschoolers up to age 5?

A. Curriculum? I meet questions like this all over the country, and they impress upon me that I can't say too often that you homeschooling families do not need school at all for your preschoolers or kindergartners.

Curriculum for a 3-year-old? How about a loving home life that is somewhat orderly in normal household routines? Add plenty of play time which is mostly free exploration and exercise, and only sometimes guided to new activities. Add the outdoors. The yard is good. Or find some sand and sun, or stream or pond or woods. Add a few friends—of all ages.

That sounds almost perfect to me. The normal home life will include some books and reading. Somebody may teach the preschooler to print his name. He might memorize his address or phone number and learn safety procedures that are needed in his environment. He will learn to brush his teeth, to eat well and sleep regularly. Language learning? Family and friends are always teaching that. If we could list all that a child learns during these years, it would make such a long list that any formal curriculum would look paltry beside it.

All the government worries about being ready for school have to do with neglected children and dysfunctional families (or jobs and tax money). Homeschoolers, please understand that your children have the best possible start in life because they have the best of families. Don't get sucked into pushing formal learning on your preschoolers because the outer society thinks they need it. At the worst, this approach can burn children out on book learning before they ever see how exciting it is. At the best, you may enjoy some curricular activities with your children and manage to keep this from harming them.

Q. What subjects do you teach first?

A. All through the preschool years you are teaching real life and real world information. You probably could find a bit of every subject in that.

But to begin what we call "school," it is helpful to think of subjects as two kinds: skill and content. Through the primary years, emphasis is on skills. Children learn to read and write the language well. Later they use these skills for learning content. That emphasis begins at about fourth grade reading level. Thus while learning to read, you can use materials with any content. Children don't need certain facts or topics; they just need to grow in the skill of reading.

The same system works somewhat in math, in that primary years are for gaining understanding of numbers and skills in basic arithmetic. Later grades build on this for topics of percentage, ratio, algebra, and so forth.

You no doubt can see the overlap in all this. You can't practice a skill without using some kind of content, and you can't learn content without increasing some skill in that area. But to answer your question, it may help to think of emphasizing skills first.

Q. Which type of readers do you recommend, phonics or basic?

A. I assume you mean the "Nan can fan" type versus the "Dick and Jane" type. I prefer the Nan-can-fan books, mainly because far more children can be successful with those.

About half of all children learn to read no matter what books you use. The other half are greatly helped if reading is simplified in the early stages, as the phonics readers are. I call it instant reading: learn a few sounds and practice them immediately. This not only reinforces the initial phonics taught, but it also introduces the system of putting sounds together to form words. The books then proceed to introduce more sounds and more practice to go with them. This gradual immersion into the complexities of English word patterns helps more children than any system I know.

But nothing works with everybody. I remember Jerry in one of my second grades. I tried my favorite methods. Tutors and classmates also tried to help Jerry get started reading. Finally I let him go across the hall to join a Dick-and-Jane reading group that was in the beginning primers. A proud and happy Jerry came back each day to read for me from his primers. I can't explain that, but it taught me not to be dogmatic about how to teach reading.

Q. When someone mentions "Ruth Beechick," I immediately think "real books." We use lots of real books, but, unlike textbooks, they do not come with discussion questions, comprehension exercises, or make-and-do projects. I'm so desperate for guidance that I've almost bought thinking skills and reading comprehension workbooks, but I know there must be a better way.

My second concern is about the projects—dioramas, posters, drama, making charts, coloring pic-

tures. I run a constant debate in my head: Is the primary value of projects in the increase of "school" knowledge or in the doing of the project? I can understand the benefits of review and retention related to a subject being studied. I can also see the benefits when a child conceives and carries out projects on his own, even if not related to any school topic. Since my children come up with lots of things to do on their own, I have been hesitant to assign time-consuming school projects. Yet I would hate to shortchange them in their education. My girls are 8 and 9.

A. First, concerning comprehension, I think that's a false issue. If your girls sit and read, they are comprehending. Who would sit with a book for more than two minutes if they weren't getting something interesting and mind-engaging out of it? And the workbook way of chopping reading into parts has not worked, according to research. So don't succumb to the workbook temptation.

Yours sounds like a family that naturally talks about books or certain happenings in them. That works better than forced school questions. Some books you need not discuss at all, others you might ask some questions to reinforce the girls' learning of the content. And some you could try having the girls narrate back to you what they read, or what you read aloud. This has additional advantages of organizing, thinking and speaking. Try these varied levels of talking about books. There is no magic school formula that will gain a higher level of thinking. Conversation with you is the best way to attain that.

Concerning projects, the same kind of variation can apply. You do a good job of explaining the values in projects, so trust your judgment on when and what to do. The importance of projects may be somewhat oversold. Lesson planners often include them simply to add some fun to the lesson. But a problem with this is that the same things aren't fun for all children. I write as one who had to endure crafts in VBS when I would rather have been memorizing more verses to earn more points.

Sounds to me like you're doing a great job. Keep following your best instincts.

Q. For teaching more than one grade level do you feel that unit studies are better than other curriculum?

A. In general, yes. Theoretically, that's one of the advantages of unit curriculums. But you'll have other considerations, too.

For instance, at primary grade levels you should focus on developing the three R's skills. But the multigrade units focus on content. At early levels of reading you are hard pressed to find enough easy books for your child, so you wouldn't want the additional problem of trying to find books on a certain unit topic. Any topic will do for reading practice.

With older grades, it works fine to have several children studying one topic. Each will naturally read and write on his own level. They can work on projects together or separately, share their learnings, go on field trips, listen to you read, and so on. Primary children can be drawn into much of this family activity, too.

Another advantage of published unit curriculums is that they usually are full of wonderful ideas. Thus they provide a lot of teacher training for you. Many homeschoolers use these for a while and then have confidence to try their own choice of unit topics. When you reach this point, then any curriculum or none will do. For instance, you may all study the topics in your sixth grade history book this year and in the fifth grade book next year.

Not only does the teacher learn from unit curriculums, so do the children. Once they know ways to display or report their learning, then you can say, "I want you to read at least three books on your topic and then share with us what you learned." I guess I like the easy route; I used to do that in classrooms and it worked wonderfully well. Part of the success, I suppose, was due to a bit of competition in the presentations. No one was going to give a dull, perfunctory report when others were being quite creative. With several children in your family, they will learn from each other and the presentations will improve over time. Inviting grandparents or other audiences helps too.

Some unit curriculum items you could purchase are simply booklets with ideas for studying one topic such as airplanes or flowers. Others are more full-blown, endeavoring to integrate what are usually separate subjects in school. History is sometimes the base of these, and the subjects of geography, science, literature, art, music and others are integrated with the study of a historical period. A study I have recently written is based on Genesis, with the humanities integrated. One prominent unit curriculum is built around themes of character traits. Mission boards are now offering materials to teach the religion, life and needs of certain areas or peoples. What a variety to choose from!

In contrast, graded textbooks are arranged with a sequence of topics that over time have become somewhat standardized in our schools. There is no reason why each of your children at home needs to study the U.S. colonial period in fifth grade and ancient empires in sixth grade.

Yes, for the content subjects, unit studies generally better fit a family lifestyle of learning.

Q. Will my child be missing basic skill stuff if I have my second grader and fourth grader doing fourth grade history and science together? What should I expect from my second grader when using this approach?

A. No, the second grader is not likely to miss basics; he's more likely to get a richer dose of them. I will add a few sentences of reasoning behind this answer. Scope and sequence plans are simply a convenience for running school districts and selling textbooks. They do not lay out a route that every child must follow lest he be inadequately educated. No such route can ever be devised, because learning does not happen in such a linear fashion. There's no necessity to study stars before magnets, or ancient Egypt before colonial America. Either order will work fine.

About including the younger child, realize that this planning problem is somewhat easier than planning separate topics for each child. some ideas are: he reads easier books on the topic, the older child reads some materials to him, he participates in or listens to conversations of teacher and older child, he does projects and writing within his ability, he helps the older child on more difficult projects, he watches videos and understands what he can from them. That's the general idea. You and the children will think of more activities as you go along.

Q. I am a homeschool mom of five years. Our approach is very creative, non-traditional, unit study, libraryish. The reason for my letter is this. I am burned out! I don't want to do wonderful projects anymore. I would rather go out for coffee with the ladies. I'm not interested in motivating my boys, 8 and 10, for math. I would rather send them to the table with something—anything that I don't have to help them with.

I have always been very much against the canned curriculum approach, but now it seems very tempting. (Possibly even public school.) The problem with always making everything fun and creative is that when I need the boys to do some serious, plain old disciplined work, they fight it. I would appreciate your advice; we are not getting very much accomplished these days.

A. Your question arrived in February, and you sound just like several of the moms in the support group that met at my home last evening. My first response is that February or March is normally the burnout season, for classroom teachers as well as home teachers. So change the pace or take a vacation or do whatever you can to get through this. And don't make major decisions until later. The burnout could have happened with any curriculum or schooling plan you might have been following.

Going through a period like this doesn't blow your whole school year. Realize that learning doesn't happen in specified, measured bits per day. A lot of it happens in spurts, and your boys just aren't spurting right now.

My second response is to comment on the curriculum concerns in your letter. It sounds as if you are working hard at being a creative teacher and, right now at least, the boys are not responding in kind. It is a lot of work to pre-plan units or other lessons; that's why homeschool publishers have a place in this enterprise. You could use any such materials that you like, and if you keep control by choosing what and when and how much, you need not feel that you have fallen into a "canned curriculum" approach.

Publishers of unit studies, some of them at least, work out in great detail the activities, the topics to learn, books to use and so forth, and if you are trying to do that on your own, it's no wonder you are feeling burned out. I didn't do that much work when I taught units. A unit can be as simple as the child himself choosing a topic, finding books at the library, reading what he wants to in them, and reporting at the dinner table some interesting stuff that he learned. During the school years of exploring topics, some will be mildly interesting, some few will be exciting, and occasionally one will become a lifelong interest. We can't expect each school day to throb with excitement.

Try paring back your expectations to what creativity the boys might show, instead of what you have been showing. Find ways to encourage and support any bit of initiative on their part, and take pleasure in any growth you see along this line.

And if sometimes you just send them to the table to do their math without you, that's okay. You don't have to constantly motivate. Motivation, interest, discipline—these all are traits that you want to build within your boys. And, like the academic subjects, these are only partially developed now. But your own intense effort and discipline will pay off; these boys will reach college age being young men that you are proud of. At that time you'll look back, and the burnout periods will be a dim memory.

Q. My husband and I are both bilingual. I feel that English is my first language, but for my husband Spanish is first. To create a bilingual learning environment for our children ages 2 and 4, I have established certain days as English or Spanish only days. Concepts such as colors, shapes, Bible stories, etc. are first taught in English. Once I feel they understand the concept I repeat it in Spanish.

Thus far this has worked out beautifully. However my 4-year-old has been asking for the last year to learn to read. Without realizing it I began to work with him early (games, reading to him, asking him to repeat or narrate stories, etc.). He can now distinguish many sounds (including blends) in both languages. I can read him a story in one language and he can narrate back what he understood in the other language. I would like to continue with the system I've successfully used, however because of my husband's opposition to doing this I am apprehensive about trying to teach reading in two languages.

Would I be hurting my children by trying to teach them in two languages, or would I be enriching their learning experience?

A. First, I should say that I am inexperienced in bilingual education, and I find little consensus among educators about the best approach. The constant debates seem more related to money and bureaucracies than to research about what works. So my opinion comes from my work as a reading specialist and from some cases of missionary families and foreign adoptions that I know of.

From that perspective, I'll begin by saying that your husband has a point. When a young child learns letter-by-letter how to read, we usually add skills in spelling, writing, punctuation and so forth, so that it is all quite complicated, and for some children almost overwhelming. But for an older child who already reads and writes in one language, learning to read in his second language is not all that difficult.

So it seems best to me to continue as you are with oral language development in both languages, but to begin reading instruction only in one. Then when your son is about fifth grade or 10 years old, and a good reader, begin reading in the second language. It may surprise you how quickly it goes. In fact, if he retains his present attitude of begging for reading, he may just teach himself from books that are lying around.

I congratulate you for your foresight and good planning to develop two languages and keep them alive in your children. By starting so young, they will speak both languages without the accents they would have if you had waited.

Q. *We started our study of history by reading aloud to our boys (ages 9, 7, and 6) from your book* Adam and His Kin. *My oldest son had been dreading history because he had heard from friends that it was boring. So what a blessing to overhear him tell his friends that history was great and we were reading this "awesome" book. When we were done, one of our younger sons asked when we could begin* Abraham and His Kin. *Are you writing such a book? If not, could you suggest some other historical books similar to this for us to read?*

A. No, I don't plan to write *Abraham* but it's surprising how often I am asked this question. I think it shows that many homeschoolers have caught on to the idea that history is the story of mankind on this earth, and textbooks too often lose the story or omit the interesting parts. When God tells history in the Bible, it is largely story.

Several homeschool suppliers have compiled lists of good books to use for learning history. Greenleaf Press* has done this perhaps as systematically as anyone. To continue the Bible story where *Adam* leaves off, you might want to look at *The Book of God* by Walter Wangerin, Jr. This is called "The Bible as a Novel," and it keeps events more connected than typical Bible story books do.

*Greenleaf Press, 3761 Hwy 109N Unit D, Lebanon TN 37087. Phone 615-449-1617. E-mail: Greenleaf@aol.com.

Q. What do you think of following E.D. Hirsch's core curriculum recommendations?

A. I think exactly as E.D. Hirsch does about shared cultural core curriculum. Here is a brief quote from his introduction to *The Dictionary of Cultural Literacy.*

> We also hope and expect that no one will be willing to stop with cultural literacy as a final educational aim. Cultural literacy is a necessary but not sufficient attainment of an educated person. *Cultural literacy is shallow; true education is deep.* [Emphasis mine.]

That total essay in the introduction is a wonderful statement of what reading and literacy are all about. It counterbalances the advertising hype that bombards you with the message that more phonics teaching can solve our nation's illiteracy problems. It can't.

So, with Hirsch's attitude that cultural literacy is necessary but not sufficient, go ahead and use the listed items as he would like them used. That is, don't memorize them as so many history dates. But use them to alert you to areas of knowledge you think your children should be more familiar with. If you see Aesop's fables listed and realize that your children have never read any, then enjoy a book of these stories, and try to follow up by comparing a couple of them to later life situations. Is someone crying "Wolf"? Does someone show a sour grapes attitude? Get acquainted, understand, enjoy. At older ages study some items in depth, but this is not a course to pass for certification as a culturally literate person.

In Hirsch's research, the Bible was shown to be the most widely known book. He wrote, "No one in the English-speaking world can be considered literate without a basic knowledge of the Bible." Items from the Bible alone take twenty-five pages in his original dictionary, whereas items from all of mythology and folklore together take only eighteen pages. Comparison with other categories shows a similar dominance of the Bible.

But after committees of teachers sorted the items into grade level books, I don't see the same proportion of Bible items. I mention this so you won't be tempted to slight Bible study in order to fit in other cultural stuff.

Q. I bought the textbooks that my friend recommended, but I don't like them as well as she does. For one thing, we continued school for weeks into the summer until my husband had his vacation, and we still didn't cover everything. What are we doing wrong?

A. This idea of covering a subject causes lots of

frustration. I wish I could remove the word from education writings. Thinking this way tends to make us slaves to the textbooks. Our attention is on the book and on pulling or pushing our students through it, instead of focusing our attention on the students and their expanding minds, and helping them find ways to expand further.

Publishers always put more than enough into their textbooks because they can't have teachers complaining that they run out of material before the semester end. Many teachers simply go as far as they can and leave the last chapter(s) undone. Other teachers manage to finish by skipping or skimming quickly over chapters that they like less or that they consider less important for their students.

Here are more thoughts to help free you from textbook slavery. The prime powers moving the textbook industry are money and marketing. Other powers are various political and societal and education pressure groups. Not all are necessarily negative from our Christian point of view, but some are. Then the books themselves are written by committees, or by ghost writers under the direction of committees or of big-name experts. This entire process empties them of any author personality or viewpoint or other features that make up what we call real books. These are non-book books.

Good teachers use supplementary material to make their courses interesting. They use only what they want to from the textbook, and that amount can vary greatly, depending on the course and on the teacher. In history, particularly, almost everybody agrees that the textbooks are dull. They try to include too many topics, so they skim over the surface and can't take space for the stories and human interest that would make the material interesting and memorable. Much that is interesting in history is now too controversial politically, so it gets pushed out by the pressures mentioned above.

In science, too, something is terribly wrong with our textbook system of "covering" topics. Research shows that young children have great curiosity about science and learn a lot from life and home and television or wherever. But in school their interest and their test scores progressively deteriorate, so that by high school level only a small percentage of students still study science with interest. At the time of this writing the national push to cure this is to require of all students more of the same failing system.

I'm glad you quit the textbooks when your husband had his vacation. I imagine that your children learned a lot from time spent with him or from your trip or whatever they did with their time once they were emancipated from textbooks.

Q. I have been homeschooling for five years now and am getting more and more discouraged. My son 9 and daughter 6 find school a drudgery.

I was using curriculum but found that it required too much from the student and the mom. I am trying to make unit studies using a history and science book on their age level but still find that their enthusiasm has evaporated, and frankly so has mine.

I am headed for burnout trying to find the best way to interest them.

My son likes science and experiments. My daughter has a short attention span and would rather play with her dolls. Am I dealing with laziness or am I not working hard enough?

A. To take your last question first, I would say you're certainly working hard enough—if anything, too hard. And I would not suspect laziness. I don't recall ever knowing a child as young as yours that I would characterize as lazy. Once I nagged one of my sons for just sitting and not doing anything, and later I found out that he was sick.

It is unnatural for healthy children to be lazy. And we must remember that much thinking and learning is invisible to us. A child can sit and think, or play with dolls and learn. While your daughter is engrossed with doll play her mind is busy growing in numerous ways. And by the way, what is her attention span when she plays with dolls? Would you say she has a short attention span if this were the measure?

From your figures it appears that you began homeschooling when your son was 4, which was unnecessary. (See the preschool chapter.) So you can loosen up for a time now to make up for those extra years.

I posed your question to a support group meeting in my home. Rita, a veteran of several years like you, said, "One thing you can tell her is to lay off the 6-year-old. Let her play with dolls. She can do a little schoolwork in short spurts."

Other ladies suggested: 1) letting the children choose their own topics, 2) lifting time pressures of too many schedules and goals, and 3) planning ways to keep up your own good attitude. On this last, Mary Ellen said she has religion study first so that she at least begins the day with her children by thinking on eternal things.

From an educator's view, it would be perfectly okay if you let your son major on his science experiements while other subjects slide for a time. Don't worry if at first his activities don't add up to units in your mind. Just give him time and see what does develop from his interests. While he reads on his topics, you could read what you enjoy and get some renewal for yourself that way.

After two or three months of a more relaxed family life, you can take a new look at curriculum. You and the children may all decide not to be so schoolish with your school as you have been.

3.
Preschool

Finding God's Plan for Your Preschoolers

Some of the most special times I will remember as a homeschooler came when my children were very young. Days filled with nature walks and reading stories aloud, the occasional art project that would fill two rooms, going to parks and building great cities with blocks. Life and learning seemed so joyous and so natural, and a pattern for our homeschooling years seemed to be forming.

This was true until I started feeling pressured to do school. At this point, things seemed to change from the setting I described above to one of stress and struggle and even resistance. While my son, in particular, did what was required of him, he once told me in all seriousness that he would read for me when he had to, but he didn't want to read for fun anymore. I was devastated. How could this happen to MY child—the one who just months before had seen learning as a great adventure?

I found the answer through reading Ruth's books and talking with her. The problem wasn't my son, the problem wasn't even me. The problem lay in understanding God's timetable for my son. When I prayed in this way, I found that we could proceed with teaching and learning, but my understanding of what school should be for my young children had to change. I couldn't even assume that what was right for my son would be right for my daughter. We had to seek God for what approach to use with her, and what his timing was to suit her particular strengths and weaknesses, gifts and talents.

With so many different approaches to preschool and kindergarten out there today, Ruth's words will seem refreshingly clear and peace-giving. Read on as she answers questions on a subject she knows well—understanding and explaining what to do with preschoolers.

—*Debbie*

Q. What would you do with a 3-year-old?

A. I would just live everyday family life with the child, and not worry about doing any formal schooling. Preschool specialists almost unanimously agree that home is the best place for preschoolers to live and grow. We have preschools for political reasons, teacher-union reasons, and all sorts of reasons except for the best interests of the child.

If you are homeschooling older siblings the solution is somewhat different, as the preschooler usually wants school along with the others. In that case, you need supplies of clay, blocks, paper and crayons, tapes of stories and music, and so forth that the 3-year-old gets to use only during his school time.

Preschoolers, and kindergartners too, who live in loving families have what's called a language rich environment, much richer than in classrooms where they interact mostly with other children their age. And language development is the main purpose of preschools and kindergartens.

Below are listed ten priorities for early childhood education according to a survey of principals supervising early childhood classrooms. I don't see any priorities here that you parents can't do better than a classroom teacher can. Notice that "academic achievement" is ninth on the list of ten. Even that one doesn't have to scare you, because you'll be teaching about numbers through real life activities and you'll be teaching vocabulary and knowledge through reading to and talking with the child, and so on. The numbering in this list indicates where some items were tied in the rankings.

1. Language development.
1. Social development.
3. Emotional development.
3. Self-discipline.
5. Physical coordination and motor development.
6. Development of health and safety habits.
7. Development of work and study habits.
8. Personality development.
9. Academic achievement.
10. Artistic expression.

Q. What is your viewpoint on teaching Spanish language to 2- and 3-year-olds? There are programs for this age and up to a complete language/grammar course, and we are interested in having our children learn Spanish.

A. Spanish language should be great, especially in your state (Texas). And it may encourage you to know that homeschools have several powerful advantages over classrooms in language teaching.

Here's why. Babies are born with the ability to make every sound in every language. That's what they're practicing all those hours in the crib. But as we parents reinforce only the sounds of our language the children gradually lose ability to make the unused sounds, until at about age seven they are proficient only in the sounds of their own family's language (or two languages in a bilingual home). Then at teen age or whenever we introduce foreign language instruction, the children must struggle with pronunciation, and never fully master it. They will always speak with an accent.

Knowing this, which is all well established by research, the ideal approach is to begin early with letting your children hear and say something in Spanish. Nursery rhymes, songs and such are good if the model is a native speaker of Spanish, either live or on tape. A little of this through the years should keep the pronunciation ability alive until whatever age you want to proceed with more serious study.

The idea in teaching a modern language these days is to let children learn it in the natural, oral way that they learn their first language. And it's amazing how much grammar a child knows by age 5, or even 3. So with your young children don't make the language difficult and dull by studying grammar. Just stick with the fun stuff they put out these days on tapes and videos and picture books.

Q. What do you recommend for a 4-year-old who wants to be able to read?

A. I would read to him and enjoy books together. I'd stop sometimes for him to fill in a key word or a rhyming word or repeated line. I'd let him say any parts along with me or repeat after me. I'd let him tell what he thinks will happen next. I'd occasionally point out to him the beginning letter of a word, such as the sound that his own name begins with. I'd leave books where he can reach them and use them by himself.

All those and similar ideas are informal, cuddly activities that families often do without even thinking "school." And that's enough reading to do with most 4-year-olds. Read the next answer with its cautions on too much book work.

Q. If my son is reading at age 4, should I let him go for it?

A. You do not need to deny your son all reading and make him wait because of hearing that it's better late than early. Let him read what he will, and answer his questions.

But some cautions are in order for physical

reasons. For one, at age 4 your son's eyes should not be subjected to much close work. Limit his reading to a few minutes at a time. For another, written work like a phonics workbook page may be a problem because many children have not developed their hand preference by this age, and you should not force this preference early or make the selection yourself.

So, I'd say that the best course for a child like this is to do what you naturally would do as a mother, and don't start formal school lessons in reading.

Debbie's Note: When my daughter was four, she told me she wanted to learn to read, and though I felt it was early, I decided to try teaching her a few sounds, and used a little book called a Bob Book. It was small, and used mainly words made with the three or four sounds they taught in that book. When we were done, and she had figured out how to read the words in that book, I told her we would do some more learning about reading tomorrow. She looked at me with very big eyes and said, "But I just wanted to learn how to read one book." I laughed to myself, realizing that even she knew she wasn't ready for daily, formal reading instruction. She carried her one book around with her for quite a while, reading it to any interested party, completely satisfied with her ability to read.

Q. *What is the best thing to do for a kindergartner who is bored because his third and fourth grade sisters take so much longer to do school?*

A. The best source of ideas for this is other homeschooling moms, either at your support group or in books written by moms. There are a number of good ones available from home-school suppliers. One idea that moms use is to have boxes or shelves of differing materials. One box may include crayons and paper and such for coloring time. Then that gets put away and a box with puzzles gets used for a while, and so on. Snack time, outdoor play time, story time with an older child reading to the kinder-gartner, and nap time all give a little structure and variety to the day.

Some other moms work on the premise that it is not up to them to plan the child's full day. If the child says, "I'm bored," then the mom says, "Well, you can wash the dishes." When you use this system, the child learns some old-fashioned free play. He develops initiative and creativity and thinking. Of course you need safety rules and noise rules. And you need to give the child his share of attention and lap time. I like this latter system better. Besides the advantages to the child, it makes life easier for you and other family members, both now and in the future.

Q. I'm not a teacher, so I need lots of help choosing curriculum and lots of help from the curriculum. I would like to start with a preschool-kindergarten curriculum to get my feet wet. I also have two toddlers to keep entertained.

A. I suggest, first, that you try to change your thinking from the entertainment idea to some-thing more like training. If you train your children, including toddlers, concerning what they are allowed to play with around the house, and how to put things away, this is curriculum. Train them to help in any household chores that they can manage at their young ages. As I mentioned in the preceding answer, many good ideas are written in the books by homeschooling moms. Let your children set the table for lunch, sing or recite a grace, eat and talk about God's provision, about nutrition, and about anything else, say Please and Thank You, and have the children help clean up afterward. View all these little matters as curriculum.

If you have errands to do, that all becomes curriculum too. Add naps, bathtub play, outdoor play, indoor play, story time, drawing or scribbling, and some music, both listening and singing (and rhythmical movement), and you have a very full curriculum. Don't overlook the fact that you are conversing with your children during much of this time and that is important for their language development. If you could manage a visit to a preschool or kindergarten someday, you would realize that your curriculum at home is rich indeed. I can't seem to say often enough that our middle class families do not need kindergarten at all.

If you still want to get your feet wet with books, try an idea given by homeschool writer, Cathy Duffy. She suggests buying workbooks from the grocery store. These are not too long, as an official curriculum for the kindergartner may be.

If getting your feet wet means getting ready for first grade, I will add that you need make no drastic change for age 6. Children do not change drastically at that time. At story time your oldest child will simply be recognizing more of the words; at drawing time, he will be writing more labels or sentence captions for his pictures, and so on. You can ease gradually into any book work that you want to add.

Debbie's Note: Several years ago, I had to take a course in early childhood education to maintain that area on my teaching certificate. Since this was an undergraduate level course, the teacher was preparing the students who were to become teachers of young children, probably as their first experience teaching. The curriculum that was being taught as the best for preschoolers was astonishing to me, not because of it's difficulty, but because it was exactly what most children would normally do every day. The curriculum was basically to recreate home life.

A corner of the classroom was to be devoted to kitchen play (complete with miniature sinks, stoves and refrigerators), a corner with dress-up clothes for make-believe, a corner with books for quiet reading, a listening center where children could listen to tapes or watch videos, and then an area for free play which included toys like blocks and cars. They would use an area of the room for sand and water play, or painting and art. The teachers were to plan the day with time for snacks, lunch and outdoor play. Except for the fact that all the materials are not out at once, I realized that the main goals of a good preschool were the same kinds of things done in most homes by stay-at-home moms, and that the quality preschool education they were talking about was just an attempt to duplicate a home with interested and caring family members.

Concerning the issues of getting along with

others, taking turns, etc., I again realized these were addressed daily in our home, and with a manageable number of children. Often the behavior problems children have in preschool are because of the lack of individual attention from adults. I came away from that class knowing that homeschoolers never need to feel inadequate regarding the educational opportunities they provide for their preschoolers.

Q. *I love having my daughter, 4 years old, at home, so I'm thinking of homeschooling her for kindergarten next year. But I worry that she'll miss out on the socialization with other children. She has two younger siblings to play with, but won't she need the kindergarten experience? If I homeschool her, how can I be sure she won't miss anything?*

A. No, no and no. Don't send your daughter to school for socialization. No, she doesn't need the kindergarten experience. No, she won't miss anything.

I'll hedge on one of the no's. She will miss a few things. She'll miss learning aggressive and other undesirable behaviors from peers at school. She'll miss learning some words you'd rather she never hear. And possibly music, too. She'll miss being exposed to the illnesses of thirty other families. She'll miss daytime hours away from you. If it's an academic kindergarten she's not going to, she'll miss losing an important characteristic called "disposition to learn."

I can't say often enough that middle class families do not need kindergarten or preschool. Ever since their origins in Europe, kindergartens and preschools were planned mainly to help neglected children, usually from poor, inner-city families. Today, preschools are growing in the way that all bureaucracies grow. That is, if they can get all children enrolled, then the unions get more teacher jobs, union leaders get more money and power, schools get more government money (your money, remember), administrators have bigger jobs and thus bigger salaries, and so on. The excuse always is "for the good of the children," but don't believe that.

Research that shows negative results from moving young children out of the family and into the classroom doesn't get media attention, and there is plenty of such research. Occasionally some research obtains positive results, and that gets the media hype. But those results are obtained from spending huge amounts of money trying to rescue children from what we call at risk environments. For instance, in Headstart they get better results when they have parent involvement. Surprise! What better way to get more government funding? This war continues pressing on many fronts. They may confiscate your money, but don't let them confiscate your child.

Since there are no benefits to gain from school for your young child, then there's no point in imitating school at home. Train your daughter to behave properly. Let her participate in family activities. Let her play a lot. And do the normal teaching that you would as a parent if you had never heard the word *homeschooling*. You'd teach her to pronounce words correctly, you'd teach her to print her name and a few other words, you'd enjoy books with her, and so on. You'd converse with her and not even think that was teaching, but that's where her best language development comes from.

There's no scheduling and hurrying. There's no formal curriculum. Just live out what Debbie calls God's plan for your daughter.

4.
Reading

Johnny *CAN* Learn To Read, And With Me as his Teacher!

Teaching your child to read is one of the most awesome experiences a parent can have. The sense of joy and accomplishment you feel ranks right up there with watching your child's first step, or hearing his first word. The first time your child actually reads a word like *star*, instead of struggling to sound it out, you will probably be amazed and overwhelmed. I know I was. As a classroom teacher, I was often the one privileged to witness this miracle of reading. Now you as a homeschooler can experience this exciting leap forward in your child's development. But with the blessing can also come a sense of responsibility that may become burdensome.

This worry about reading is common among homeschoolers. Many times, our very existence as homeschoolers seems to hinge on our children gaining this important skill. Husbands want our children to read, grandparents want to see (and hear) our children read, and even the government wants us to prove our children can read. So we resort to strange, yet understandable, approaches to address this situation. We buy expensive phonics programs. We start teaching our children early so that they will have a head start (or maybe just learn it by the time everyone else does). We fret and often push our children until they feel as much stress as we do. The reason for this scenario is that we care very much about giving our children the best education we can. We don't want them to be shortchanged in any way, and we especially don't want to be the cause of their lack of achievement.

It is in this situation that Ruth's advice is so freeing. The following answers for some common questions can help you go from stressing out to having the attitude of a patient gardener—watering, weeding and waiting for God's timing for the fruit.

—Debbie

Q. Is it possible to start teaching reading too late?

A. As far as ability to learn the reading, it's never too late. The usual argument given against a late start is that the child will miss out on learning during those years or months in which he doesn't read. But I don't buy that argument; it assumes that all learning comes from books. I can counter with the argument that the child misses out on learning during all the extra time spent trying to learn phonics and reading if he begins too early. In fact, I can cite research which bears this out. At the optimum time, children learn more quickly and easily than at too early a time.

Children who learn to read at 9 or at 12, usually learn quickly. These are often cases where it took until then to overcome some sort of neurological problem which made reading difficult earlier. These children do not slowly work their way through first grade books, then second grade books, and so forth. Instead, they quickly read at whatever level they are at in thinking, vocabulary and knowledge. So they are not permanently behind as a result of a late start.

In our times, the main problem with a late start is the psychological hurt the child must endure from the pressures of peers and society. This is severe in the schools and less severe among homeschoolers, who usually do a wonderful job of bringing these children successfully through the difficult non-reading years. In fact, this is one of the greatest contributions you homeschoolers make to elementary education in our society. Society doesn't appreciate it, though. You must accomplish this with relatives and government officials looking over your shoulders, and in the face of your own fears and uncertainties.

The homeschool movement has within it and around it a growing number of services and information directed toward these late-start readers. I pray that each of you will find the support and help you need.

Q. I've just finished my first year, kindergarten, and I'm using the "later is better" method. But I seem to stand alone among friends and support group. What advice do you have?

A. "Later is better" is not exactly the teaching of people who warn against starting too early. Dr. Raymond Moore's book is titled *Better Late than Early*, and it documents the dangers of pushing for too early a start. I often speak of an optimum starting time, which is the time in each child's life when he is able to catch on to some beginning reading skills.

So on the one hand, you need not delay a child who is eager to read, and on the other, you should not push a child who doesn't seem ready. With friends, try talking about other things your son is doing, instead of talking about where he is in reading.

Q. When do I move to harder books? Now my kindergartner is reading primers like, "I see the dog run."

A. Europeans call this "the American question." As soon as we Americans label some steps, we push and pull our children up the steps as early and as rapidly as possible. But this is a mistake. It's far better to richly experience each step before moving on. This is true in beginning reading as elsewhere. I realize that you have a problem finding a lot of books at the see-the-dog level, but it's worth the effort to find what you can. Concurrently with that reading, you could occasionally point out a phonics element on the words your child knows, usually an initial consonant, as *see* begins with the same sound as her name *Sally*.

Q. *I have a 5 1/2-year-old who reads quite well at about the second or third grade level. He is the very independent type. We used your "non-method" method, if you'll excuse me calling it that. It was very successful! But now he doesn't want me to read with him because I try to teach him if he needs help as we go along, using a phonics rule system that both he and his brothers are familiar with. I'm a little concerned about syllabication and reading longer words. He figures out quite a bit from context and recognizing words that he has read before. I feel like he knows just enough phonics to get by with, but that later on he will suffer from not having the skills he needs to decode longer words. He isn't motivated to learn more (at least now). What is your advice?*

A. Since your son has done so well for his age, I think you can forget even the little concern that you have about his future reading. I imagine that he is enjoying the first flush of success, and this is why he prefers to read on his own and not be burdened with new learning. Perhaps, also, he needs time to consolidate the skills he already has and become fluent with them. In this case, pushing ahead with new skills would amount to overload. Also, too much time with close bookwork may damage his eyesight at this young age. So there are several reasons to relax and let him be for now.

Do you think he objects to the phonics help because it interrupts the thoughts he is reading about? You can usually tell the boy any words he needs and teach the phonics later in a spelling or writing lesson. But he's only 5, remember. You could forget the teaching for now. Children who easily begin reading pick up much phonics information on their own. If they figure out *light* from *right*, for instance, that is phonics. They are seeing the patterns that we call phonics rules. We don't have to teach it all for them to learn it all.

As for syllabication, I think some curriculums emphasize this far too much. As an editor I am one of the few people in the world who have to get this right, and I usually do it with a dictionary by my side. Over the next couple of years you no doubt will be able to teach your son enough of both syllabication and phonics. I'd say you can quit worrying while he is 5.

Q. I have worked through two-thirds of [a reading and phonics book] with my son over the last school year. He recently turned 6. He does well but the decoding is still very slow and he gets easily distracted. It takes two and one-half hours to do one lesson. Is this just age and exposure or should I use a different method?

A. If it's possible to diagnose at such a distance, I would say that this certainly sounds like a case of beginning phonics too soon. I suggest waiting until your son can understand and do the lessons more easily. He can use the hours saved for activities in which he experiences success. This will build confidence in his abilities and avoid burnout in reading and phonics. The phonics will be easier later on.

Q. Is it okay to first read your child's story from

the phonics reader and then have him read it to you?

A. My first thought is that it would be better to read something else to the child—a library book, a Sunday school paper, or a different kind of beginning reader. Save the Nan-can-fan reader until the child is able to figure out the words for himself. When those books work as planned, children have the high mental excitement of discovering and using patterns in English. So I wouldn't be in a hurry to teach them by word memory instead.

But my second thought is that you can do anything that seems to help your child. Just be sure you are not pushing unduly. There is plenty in the real world to learn if you delay reading for a bit.

Q. When do children stop confusing b, d, *and* p?

A. The age varies, of course, but these letters should be mastered sometime during the phonics stage of reading. We need to understand how normal this confusion is. If we hold up a fork and ask "What is this?" young children can answer, "Fork." If we turn it upside down the answer is still fork. But with these letters the answers differ according to which way we turn them.

If this is still a problem with your child, try teaching just one letter at a time. Instead of teaching how *b* and *d* face opposite directions (although some people have success using the word *bed*), teach just the *d* for a few days or few weeks. Have your child write short words that begin or end with *d*. Have him think of words that begin or end with that sound. After he has *d* well learned, then teach some other letters, and then turn to *b*.

The idea is to keep the letters separated as much as possible while the child learns each one alone. Patience and practice should eventually solve this problem.

Q. *Does it frustrate the reader who is developing his own system to be taught phonics? Does it slow down his learning?*

A. Anything that you can actually teach the child will help. But be aware that if you're following a systematic phonics program, most children take in what they are ready for and the rest will "spill over." So for a child developing his own system, you may get further by teaching phonics incidentally. That means when he asks about a word, you take the opportunity to teach the initial sound or any one phonics item that will help him figure it out. Incident by such incident you teach him phonics that doesn't spill over.

Q. *How do you help a child who reads by memorizing words rather than sounding out words?*

A. I don't think that memorizing words should be viewed as a problem. It is one technique that children use, some more than others. And it gradually gets merged with phonics. When a child figures out *take* from the word *make*, or *should* from *would*, he is using phonics. This may not be the order you were going to teach it, but it works anyway.

You don't have to worry that he'll go to college with thousands of memorized words and no word attack skills. The memory burden would have grown too heavy long before that.

Q. *What phonics program would you recommend as best for a 7-year-old boy who is disinterested in phonics. He is hard for me to motivate in this area.*

A. I believe that it matters little which program you use. I just suggest that you find an inexpensive one, unless you have money to burn. And I suggest not being a slave to it.

Instead of trying to interest your son in phonics, work at interesting him in reading itself. Read aloud from books that he likes, leave books lying around in the bathroom and other available places. You didn't say how much your son reads, but if he reads anything at all you could lay off phonics for a while and encourage reading of easy books for a few months. Later on, if he still needs phonics, he will learn it more easily and quickly. So that will be easier on you, too.

Q. *My 7-year-old son is a slow reader. He reads three-letter words at 35 words per minute maximum. He can read larger words but it is slow reading. His 5-year-old brother has passed him in speed though not in word difficulty yet.*

My husband is very frustrated with his slow progress and says if he doesn't show improvement soon maybe it's best if we send him to school. I think that would be a mistake. Any advice? Should we have him tested for any reading disabilities and if so, where do we go for that?

He does very well in his other subjects, especially arithmetic where he excels.

A. Oh no! Don't panic yet. I see the early-start mentality of our society about to pressure another family into a wrong decision. It may help to know that there is much research to show that a good average age for boys to start reading is 7 1/2. Many children now are starting later than that and doing very well academically, thanks to the homeschooling movement.

Children begin reading at later-than-average ages for many reasons, including slower physical or neurological development and slower mental development. In all these cases nothing is gained by trying too hard to speed up the reading development. That just discourages a child, damages his self-confidence, and takes the joy out of reading.

But your son doesn't appear to be a late starter. If he is reading three-letter words he already has a good beginning in phonics. I wouldn't worry about speed at this time. Just provide as much easy reading material as you can find. Admittedly it's difficult to find a lot of material at the cat-in-the-hat stage, but that is exactly what you need to do. Find the books and let him read. At his own speed. Tell him the sight words he needs—like *was*. With plenty of this easy reading, your son will become more fluent with both the decoding skills and the sight words. He may have a slight neurological problem that makes sounding out the words hard work for him. Give him time.

The next phonics level is putting two consonants together, as in *scat* or *cast* or *cats*. About half the children can't do this until well into third grade, or age 8. I have found that I can't speed up this ability by drill and memory and such. Though a child may memorize some of these with hard work, it's better to wait until his mind is ready to understand the consonant blends. That's the main hurdle in phonics. After that, the rest is easy.

So you're right on target with the way about half of all children learn to read. Among the other half are those who catch on quickly and those who have various learning difficulties. As parents, you naturally worry about whether your son will lose out somehow by not being among the faster ones. The answer is *no.* Some children have conquered reading at 10 or 12 or even later, and almost immediately their reading level is right up with their mental level. At those ages they do not slowly go through second grade books, then third grade books and so on, as younger children do.

Your main job now is to not discourage your child, not burn him out on reading, and keep up the joy of learning through other means—real life, videos, etc. Two or three years from now you will wonder why you worried.

Q. I have a second grader just now beginning to read fairly well. Do you see reading as a process of development or does it spurt when a child is ready? Is a slow starter usually always slow?

A. I see reading, and all skill learning for that matter, as occurring in spurts. And, no, a slow starter is not always slow. I don't think of second grade as particularly late. Especially if this child is a boy, this is quite average. There are many reasons why a child might not read well at the age the government thinks he should, and most late starters quickly move up to a reading level that matches their mental level and vocabulary level, so they are not forever behind because of starting later. A few of the children are later than average because their mental level is lower than average. These children have no catching up to do; they are already learning as well as we should expect.

Q. How long should I continue to have my child read out loud? When should I encourage him to read to himself silently?

A. Decide this not by age or grade, but rather by the stage of reading your child is in. Through the phonics stage, much reading will be oral because you need to hear whether your child sounds out the words correctly. You can gradually taper off the oral reading as the child becomes more competent in using phonics.

Following phonics, comes the stage for building fluency. On average this will encompass the full two years of second and third grades. In this stage the child should do a great deal of silent reading of easy material, not pushing through grade level textbooks. You will want to hear him read aloud sometimes so you can hear how he's doing, so you can help with proper pronunciation and expression, and so you can converse with him about the books. The child will see the need for good oral reading if you use it in family Bible reading times or audience occasions of reading and reciting poems, plays and other selections.

There naturally is much overlap here. While the phonics stage begins with mostly oral reading and the fluency stage is mostly silent reading, you can use either mode at any time. Silent reading can begin as early as children read anything. Let your children read silently whatever and whenever they will. You need not worry whether they skip words or read them wrong; those problems will correct as their skill grows.

The rationale behind moving into silent reading as children are able is that too much oral reading tends to develop slow word-by-word reading habits that are hard to break later on when students want to read faster. Also, they will accomplish a lot more reading if they do it silently rather than always reading to you.

Q. Do you think children should be read to once they can read by themselves? Is there an age limit on when you should stop reading aloud to your children?

A. No age limit. Continue to read aloud once children read by themselves. This is the standard advice among reading teachers for a number of reasons. Among them is that the children should not feel punished for learning to read, they can listen to more advanced books than they can read themselves, and they still gain from this sharing of the pleasure of reading.

At all ages people read aloud; there is no age to stop. Poetry, particularly, needs to be read aloud. And plays. Scripture too. And any book that you can all enjoy together. Sometimes the children participate; it's not always you reading. But as mentioned in the preceding answer, they should do more silent reading than oral reading. In classrooms the teacher read-aloud time is usually the students' favorite time of day even into the teen years.

Debbie's Note: Reading aloud has been one of the cores of our homeschooling life. Even now, my 14-year-old and 11-year-old genuinely look forward to the time each day when I read aloud to them. I keep a stack of index cards by my chair, and when we read a word that is new to the children I write it down on a card, and later one of us will write the definition on the back. Every couple of days, I pull out the stack of cards and review the words by turns, asking the children to give the definitions that they remember. This is a gradual way to build vocabulary, without using dull workbooks. The children don't seem to mind reviewing the cards, and they also learn the meanings of the words in the context of the story we are reading.

The practice of reading aloud has been a part of our unit studies since the children were very small. We have always read a book, either fiction or nonfiction, to go with every topic we have studied, and our read-aloud often forms the basis of our discussions.

The sweetest thing about our read-aloud time is that we all enjoy starting our school day this way. For many years, our devotions would begin with a read-aloud passage. Now that the children have Bible passages that they work with on their own, we use whatever book we are reading to start our day.

One morning, I was on the phone for a while before school started, and coming out into the living room I was surprised to find the children sitting on the couch waiting. I asked them why they hadn't started with their school work, and they looked at me with surprise and said we always started school together, reading on the couch. Not discerning any real attempt to avoid their work, I was touched to realize that they looked forward to our time together, listening while I read and discussing whatever topic would come from our reading.

They have often amazed me by recalling facts years later that we read aloud, so I know that learning is taking place while we read. I know that some of those times will be my fondest memories of homeschooling when my children are grown.

Q. I have a third grade son who is having difficulty in reading. He reverses some letters and numbers, but doesn't do this all the time. Should I have him tested for learning disabilities? Do you have any suggestions on how I should approach reading to make it easier for him? And me?

A. Don't be too quick to pursue testing and labels. Save that for stubborn problems that you can't solve yourself by reading or by networking among your homeschool contacts.

At third grade, with some reading trouble, I would say your son is still in the stage of building fluency in reading. So he needs to have plenty of easy material to read. If you're not providing that now, but instead are plowing through a third grade reader, this one suggestion may be all you need to make it easier on you both.

I know how people fear this idea; it doesn't seem right that children can progress better with easy material than with harder material that strains their abilities. So all I can do is keep repeating my advice and hope that you meet more parents who have used easy materials during the fluency stage and will back me up in this advice.

With easy material, your son will read more pages per day, thus getting more practice on phonics and the common sight words than he could get in the few pages of a textbook lesson. Sounding out words becomes more automatic, and not a chore. The sight words become automatic, too. And all the time the child is reading about more topics. His vocabulary and knowledge are expanding in a natural way. You don't have to force three or four new words per reading lesson, as the textbooks do; just let new words come as they may in the books you and your son choose at the library or elsewhere.

Continue this practice for a year or more, until your son reads fluently, which is about fourth grade reading level. Hopefully the reversal problem will correct itself during this process. But if it persists, see my comments on some earlier questions in this chapter.

Q. My third grade daughter tends to skip words quite often when reading orally. Should I slow her down or will this get solved on its own in time?

A. I suggest analyzing the problem a little more as to which words she skips and why. Sometimes children learn to skip words they don't know so they can get on with the story. Sometimes they have an eye problem wherein words swim around on the page, and they do the best they can, not knowing that the words sit still for everybody else. In these cases they tend to skip the function words like *the* or *all,* rather than the more colorful, substantive words. Sometimes they are fast readers, and are impatient with the pace of oral reading.

If your daughter is a good reader, and fast, I'd let her read silently most of the time, so as not to slow her down. But plan oral reading lessons occasionally, in which she practices reading something for an audience, as she needs to do in Sunday school class or elsewhere. In these sessions work on accuracy.

At third grade, your daughter is probably in the stage of building fluency in reading. That is, she knows and uses basic phonics, but now in the fluency stage she needs lots of practice with easy material. With time and practice these problems of inaccuracy should iron out.

Q. My 9-year-old son still reads some words backwards, like reading saw *for* was. *Any suggestions?*

A. Try asking him what the first letter is and what the first sound is, covering the rest of the word if necessary. Then read the word. If the reversals persist after a few weeks of attention to initial sounds, then you could take this as a clue that he may have some kind of problem with mixed left-right dominance, and you could pursue information and treatments for this condition. Some information is given in the chapter on testing and special education.

Q. *How does one deal with all the reading expected in the fourth grade when the 10-year-old boy is not reading fluently nor is interested in doing so. Also his spelling is strictly phonetic.*

A. A major advantage of homeschooling is that you can ignore grade levels. No school can magically make every 10-year-old work at a particular level. Since your son is still in the fluency stage of reading, let him read lots of easy books. Focus on building fluency in reading and don't worry if he doesn't read about Columbus or Magellan or American Indians. If you do want him to learn that kind of content, you can do it with videos or reading aloud to him.

Here's some science research that should interest you. It shows that your son will learn science better if he doesn't use science text-books. The last two international comparisons have shown Americans high in science at age 9, and lower at 13, and near bottom at 17. Now, since we begin teaching science formally at about age 9, this says that what American children learn from their environment and families and TV puts them ahead of the rest of the world in science knowledge. But when they begin formal school science their rating falls. Some analysts have concluded that we progressively turn students off to science by textbook teaching. But they are strangely silent about where the knowledge comes from before age 9; it wouldn't do to give credit to homes instead of schools.

As for spelling, it goes along with reading. A child not yet fluent in reading cannot be fluent in spelling either. If your son spells phonetically, this shows that he is thinking and trying. Give him credit for that. You can work with him on some common and useful words, one or two at a time. But save the big push on spelling until he is a more fluent reader.

Try to relax about fourth grade content subjects. Let your son learn from his real life environment and other ways. He's still learning to read. Later on he can read to learn.

Q. How do you recommend we get our seventh grade son to read and like it?

A. This simple question has no simple answer. You probably need to try several ideas, actually any promising idea that you hear of. One idea is to have a family reading time. For a set period the house is quiet and everyone in the family, including you, sits (or lies) somewhere reading his own choice of material. Another oft repeated idea is to cast around for a reading topic that interests the boy. This topic might be one of his current hobbies.

One family I know had a particular time to be in bed with lights out, but that time could be extended one hour if the child was reading in bed. A mom I know slips off to the library by herself and comes home with an armload of books. That was a new one for me, because most people are instead taking their children to the library. When the mom comes in, the children want to see what the books are, but she says, "Not now. We'll look at these tomorrow." The children feel deprived and curious and impatient to see, and by the next day they are ready to pounce on the books.

Keep trying. There's some idea out there for you.

Q. I have two boys, ages 14 and 16. Both are accomplished readers, However at times their pace seems rather slow. What sort of expectations should I require of them for completing a work of literature, especially classic literature?

A. At this age your boys could profit from a couple months practice on speed reading techniques. You will find self-teaching books on this topic from bookstores, or a course at a community college may be an option. In choosing books, it is helpful to understand two opposite approaches to speed reading that the books may advocate.

One is to push beyond your current speed, but maintain good understanding of the material. One technique for this is to slide a card down the page covering what you have just read, pushing yourself a bit, and not backing up to look at a line again.

The opposite approach is to practice techniques of moving the eyes rapidly down a page, and at first don't expect good understanding of the material. With practice, you find you can pick up more and more of the content.

Word-by-word readers go about 300 words per minute. You can test your boys' starting level by simply timing them for one minute and then having them count the words read. If they are about at this oral reading speed, a few weeks practice on some of the techniques mentioned here and in a speed-reading book should help them at least double their speed to 500 or 600 words a minute. Just two tips, alone, should accomplish that much.

Those two tips are: 1) do not ever back up to see what you think you missed, and 2) force yourself to go a little faster than speech, so you cannot mentally pronounce each word. Teenagers usually catch on to this quickly. They don't have to break the years and years of slow habits that many of us adults do.

For your boys' literature assignments the 500 to 600 range would be a good goal for books on their independent reading level (books without new words or unfamiliar content). If their current speed is slow, they should find this faster speed improves comprehension. Many writers seem surprised that that happens, but I think it is due to the higher concentration it takes to read faster.

Practicing speed reading for a while is fun. And learning to see phrases and thoughts instead of single words is stimulating. Maybe a unit on this will bring the improvement you desire.

Q. My daughter usually looks blankly at me when I ask her to tell me what she just read. How can I be sure she is comprehending?

A. Sometimes I wish we didn't have the word *comprehension*. One reason is that during the early phonics and fluency building stages of reading, children have their minds full of figuring out the sounds and staying on the right lines and other mechanical skills, and that is no time to add lessons on comprehending. There is too much silliness in teacher manuals on drawing meaning out of a sentence like, "See Spot run." The teacher's supposed to ask if Spot can run faster than Sally, why Spot is running, and so on. The real point in that sentence is whether the children can sound out the vowels and the consonants in it.

For an analogy, while I was learning to drive I wasn't critiquing the scenery. And while I was learning to type I wasn't proofing and editing and revising the content, as I do nowadays while I type.

So at the early stages of reading, I say don't bother to mix comprehension lessons with the reading. You can watch your child grow in understanding and knowledge by simple con-versation at other times of the day or by talking about books you read aloud to her. If your daughter spends time reading to herself, you know she is comprehending something. She wouldn't sit there pretending for very long. She may occasionally laugh or read a line to you, and that gives you even more visible evidence that she is comprehending. You don't need to check up story by story to act like a teacher or to keep her progress rolling along or for any other purpose that I can think of. Her reading is, itself, comprehension.

At later stages of reading, our traditional textbook-workbook system also does not treat reading sensibly. One prominent researcher wrote that we have spent decades breaking reading into bits (finding the main idea of a paragraph, choosing the best title, answering fact questions or inference questions, etc.), but the bits have not added up to the whole process of reading. Homeschoolers, at least half of them, do it right. Reading is whole with them. Sometimes for studying language or for learning to write, you could analyze paragraphs in the manner of a reading workbook. But don't spoil the wonderful joy of reading good stories and books by worrying about something called comprehension.

When children can't respond to a request to tell what they just read, it's usually not because they don't know, but because they haven't learned the skills of putting all those pages of reading into a few words. Those are speech and thinking skills. So you could work on those. In the narration system that some homeschoolers use, young children learn to tell happenings in order, and older children learn to select significant items and to relate them, and so forth.

When we first ask children to tell us about a

book, we must realize their difficulty in having an instant opinion on something they have just finished reading. They need time to digest the reading and think about what to say. And they need help for putting book thoughts into their words. If you tell your daughter what you think about some books, that supplies a model for her.

Much of the time you can be quite informal about books discussions. Ongoing conversations about books can grow naturally in a family and don't have to be profound and academic. My older son at 10 told me that Encyclopedia Brown had a drawer just to collect junk in. Why did he mention that? Did it strike some psychological need, or suggest a fun activity he could do? We couldn't afford a whole drawer, but we cleared out half a drawer where Allen could have his private junk collection. Other Encyclopedia Brown books moved him on to other thoughts and in time he outgrew those books, and our conversation on Encyclopedia Brown was over.

Nowadays we discuss books by various theologians about the rapture and other topics. The level of thinking grows as the child grows. And all along the way reading *is* comprehension.

5.
Spelling

Reducing
Spelling Problems
Down to Size

As a classroom teacher, it never failed to amaze me how children could get 100% on a spelling test on Friday, and then misspell a word from that list on Tuesday. As one child put it, "Quick Mrs. Strayer, give the spelling test. All the words are about to run out of my brain!" The methods I used as a teacher seemed to produce only short term memory of spelling words, so when I became a homeschooler, you can bet I was ready to try other methods. I came in knowing what *didn't* work.

While we worry about many different things as homeschoolers, we have certainly taken our turn worrying about spelling. This area still concerns us, even after we have made it over such hurdles as teaching our children to read or learn how to do math. Ruth's writings on spelling and her advice have helped us put spelling in its proper place.

We want our children to write well, and we all agree that communicating effectively is important, so listen as Ruth gives us practical and helpful advice on this troublesome area. The steps you take to help your children with their spelling will then be more livable and more effective.

—Debbie

Q. *Don't you need to continue through the complete phonics program to get all the spelling rules needed?*

A. If you're teaching phonics for spelling rather than for reading, I suggest looking through your program and choosing only parts that you feel are genuinely helpful for your child's spelling. Being selective will save you and your children from plowing through a lot of unnecessary, probably dull, pages. There is no magic in phonics rules that, by itself, will make your child a good speller. Phonics must be combined with several other approaches to spelling.

Q. *So, does correct spelling come naturally, without a phonics program?*

A. To say that phonics does not solve all spelling problems is not to say that spelling comes naturally. Phonics is one element in spelling. There is also a strong visual element, and a rote memory element, as well as the need for a good knowledge of English language—its homonyms, contraction rules, rules for possessives and plurals, and other grammatical rules. Spelling needs a many faceted approach.

Q. *When you have a 6-year-old who's been reading for three years and at a high level, do you need to present phonics at all?*

A. I am asked this question often. The child's age and other details vary, but the basic question is, "Is phonics something to know systematically for its own sake?" The answer is no. For young children, definitely no. Phonics is a means toward reading. If you're already at the destination, why back up to find somebody's path? The child has found his own path, and you might be surprised at how much phonics he gathered along the way, figuring out his own rules and patterns.

Some would argue that you should teach the phonics because it is also a means to good spelling. Some ads claim you can get perfect spelling by teaching phonics, but I disagree with that. There are eight ways to spell the long *e* sound, so how is a child to know which of those to use on an unfamiliar word? Every sound has several spellings. A rule of thumb about phonics spelling lessons is: If you see a lesson or rule that causes you to say, "Ah, that would have helped me," then teach it to your child.

If your child is reading well, forget phonics and move on to higher thinking. Enjoy books with him. Let him talk to you about some of his reading. And, of course, keep him surrounded with good materials to read. At his age, he probably still needs easy books to gain fluency in reading. This fluency builds a visual foundation for spelling of the common sight words, as well as for many of the phonics patterns.

Q. How do you overcome the confusion of c *and* s *in spelling?*

A. Your question provides a good illustration of the fact that phonics does not solve all spelling problems. When *s* sound is at the beginning of a word it is usually spelled *s* if the following vowel is *a, o,* or *u* (sat, sop, sup). But if the following vowel is *e* or *i,* you have a problem (cell, sell; city, sit, or cite, site). Knowing this may at least narrow your problem to words with *e* and *i* (and *y*). If the following sound is a consonant the word always begins with *s.*

As to ending positions, phonics is no help at all. Why do we spell *justice* with *c* and *promise* with *s*? This has to do with history. *Justice* is the root *just* plus the suffix *ice,* which makes the word a noun. *Promise* is the prefix *pro* (before) plus a form of the Latin *mittere* (to send). You can find all this information in any good dictionary.

Your teaching problem is to decide when to analyze the parts of a word and when to just learn its spelling. Learning historical parts often opens up whole classes of related words which you then don't have to learn one by one. But in other cases, this study can become so complicated that you'll decide it's easier to simply learn a word's spelling than to analyze its parts.

Besides phonics and word parts, a third approach to spelling is grammar. If a child knows that we form plurals by adding *s,* then he has no problem with the final sound of *cats* or *trucks*. It's always spelled *s*.

As you see, there is no quick fix for spelling. All the above skills grow with constant immersion in language activities. Read on to the next question.

Q. Please could you help me understand my daughter's problem with spelling? She was my first student and I believe I taught her the way I understood things rather than the way she learned. We began phonics at five years old and she never understood it. To me it was so logical and so we plodded along year after year until I gave up. She is also very strong willed and I thought maybe that was part of the problem. She learned to read—in fact, she would read twenty-four hours a day if she could. But her school papers are constantly, horribly, misspelled. I have taught spelling, not taught spelling, tried to be patient and see if she outgrows it, but I have great panic attacks that she will never spell. Am I too anxious about this? For her to be my daughter and not be able to spell is unthinkable.

A. You sound like many moms who ask about spelling these days. I do not think you are too anxious about this because, like it or not, our society values spelling highly. It has almost become a symbol of quality education. To project a good image of homeschooling, I think all we'd have to do is have the children write perfectly spelled letters to their grandparents and government officials.

You do not give the age of your daughter, but I suggest a more laid back approach to spelling during primary years, and a hard-work approach in later years. There are many advantages in this arrangement, which I've described elsewhere. Your daughter's case is a good illustration that early phonics training does not guarantee good spelling.

I often say that the number one spelling skill is to recognize when a word may be wrong. While writing along, every so often I say, "Oops, that doesn't look right." So I ask someone, or the spell checker. That failing, I (groan) go to the dictionary.

If you agree that spelling works something like that in real life, you could try teaching that skill. For instance, you could have your daughter go over a piece of her writing and circle every word that she is not certain is spelled correctly. In this case it is not a point off to misspell a word, it is only a point off not to circle it—if you bother with points at all. The circled words will likely suggest to you a variety of useful spelling lessons. Remember that conversation—just talking about a word—is a lesson, as is rewriting the paper to get it correct before Daddy sees it.

I asked Debbie how she would respond to these tough spelling questions, and she had a lot of good ideas which could be summed up by saying work hard and individualize. I think my suggestions could be summed up the same way.

Q. My children are through the decoding stage and fluency stage, and are now in the information stage of reading, but their spelling is poor. They love to write but sometimes the labor involved in proper spelling is discouraging. I need steps to teach good readers to be good spellers, hopefully without the drill method.

A. You have two factors already working strongly for you. First, you are past the fluency stage of reading, and that is the best time to emphasize spelling. Second, you want something more meaningful than drill.

Starting from that platform, I recommend a multifaceted approach to spelling, as I frankly don't know any simple series of steps that will do the job. My answer to an earlier question shows the complexity of just one spelling detail—when to use *s* and when to use *c* for the *s* sound. Multiply that by all the other spelling details and you build a picture of what your children must learn in the next few years.

One system I do not recommend is memorizing weekly lists of words from a spelling book. It doesn't take long for most moms to say, "My child can get 100% on Friday's spelling test, but the next week he misspells those very words in his writing." That's because the list system involves learning words in isolation from meaningful context, the most inefficient system out there.

Almost any other system besides that will contribute more to spelling improvement. Some books use a phonics approach and you can find useful materials in those. Skip what your children already know and use selected portions of such books.

Other books help you study word parts—roots, prefixes and suffixes. These are valuable, more so as children reach their teen years and can understand them better.

Besides phonics and word parts, another necessary approach is certain grammar rules. When to add *s* and *es* for plurals is one example. Related to this are rules for changing *y* to *i* before adding endings. Knowing that we add *ed* for past tense (and knowing the doubling rule) will keep a child from spelling *dreamed* as *dreamd* or *stopped* as *stopt*.

Sometimes you have no choice but to use memorizing. That's probably the best way to learn a word like *people*. Little memory tricks work. In this case, try mispronouncing it PE-o-ple.

All these curriculum approaches help: phonics, words parts, grammar rules, spelling rules, and memory. As for methods, you can use multiple approaches here too. Try to individualize as much as possible. One widely used idea is to collect words from the children's own writing. Children can learn to collect them in notebooks or on cards or wherever it works for you.

From the collections, you can devise means of studying. Sometimes form a short list of five or six words to learn. Sometimes categorize words according to a difficult phonics element or particular root, and talk about the element which will unlock for your child the spelling of those words.

Sometimes post commonly used troublesome words on a wall chart for children to refer to while they are writing. Or keep notebooks of troublesome words for children to refer to.

Anything that's faster than looking in a dictionary will reduce the labor of writing. Tell them spellings when necessary; keep the writing moving and don't let it get bogged down because of spelling.

As you start into a new unit of study, help your children compile a list of special words they will need while writing about that topic. They can collect these from the books or videos or other materials. Alphabetize this list and hang it on a wall. Don't make too fancy a poster, because this list will grow as the unit proceeds.

Multiple approaches, multiple methods, and lots of immersion in language—reading, writing and talking about it—these are the routes to good spelling. Spelling skill continues to grow throughout life. At no age or grade can we expect students to have completely mastered spelling.

Q. My 11-year-old son, who is a good reader, has a difficult time spelling sight words and remembering math facts. Yet, he can remember in other subjects. What can I do?

A. This sounds as if it's the non-meaningful items that your son has difficulty remembering, so the trick is to make them more meaningful. In math, use manipulatives, skip counting, and other activities to make the math facts meaningful and easier to visualize.

For spelling, we can define sight words as those words which use such complicated or rare phonics elements that it's easier to learn the words directly than to learn the phonics rules behind them. A good first step would be to collect for a while words that your son misses or asks for help on when he's writing, and categorize these the best you can. For instance, *would*, *should*, and *could* can be lumped together, and the three words learned with the effort ordinarily taken to learn one word.

Some phonics programs teach six sounds for *ough*, and I haven't seen them include *hiccough*, which would make a seventh sound—*hiccup*. If you remove the words with *t*, which all have the sound in *bought*, you're left with only about eighteen base words. Common sight words among these are: *through*, *though*, and *enough*. I'd say just learn those words and skip the phonics rules. From them your child will know three sounds of *ough* and can figure out most of the other words he meets*

The *wh* words usually are quite phonetic once you understand that *wh* sometimes sounds like *h* and sometimes like *hw*. For instance, *where* can be compared with *there* and *who* with *do*. *Was* is in a category all by itself. I don't know anything to do but to memorize this and similar one-of-a-kind words. Good readers usually don't have much trouble with these because they see them so often in their reading.

Tackle other categories, similarly, by analyzing and talking about them and trying to think of ways to remember them. This reasoning and mental processing strengthens the memory of the words.

*The *ough* base words, without the *bought* family and without *hiccough* are: cough, trough; bough, plough, sough, drought, doughty;

borough, thorough, though, dough, furlough; brougham, slough, through; enough, rough, tough.

Q. *My 11-year-old son has improved in spelling this year, but he was plagued with one main problem. He has trouble spelling words with a schwa in them He says he can't hear whether the sound is an e, a, i, o, or u sound. I like how he put it: "They keep ya' guessin'."*

We've already used the method of pronouncing the actual vowel sound, but it doesn't work when he is trying to compose his own work or take dictation from me. In first grade when he had a weekly list of words, he memorized them and usually made 100%.

He does have permission to use the word processor and spell checker, but I think he would enjoy being a better speller just naturally. The argument says that if a child reads a lot he will naturally spell well. That's not so with this book-devourer. We use the personal notebook idea that works by spelling and not by sound, which I think is not as successful. He likes the method all right, but the schwa remains unconquerable.

Can you suggest any other tips?

A. Here's an idea to try. Adjust the personal notebook to suit your goals, and go ahead and collect words according to schwa sound. Have your son categorize them, study, and see if he can formulate any rules. For example, take the category of *ible* and *able* suffixes which both have the same sound and the same meaning. But with a list of the words before us we could notice that soft *c* and *g* are followed by *i*. Examples: invincible, tangible. Most hard consonants are followed by *a*. Another solution to the *ible-able* problem is to see if any other suffix beginning with *i* will work (except *ing*). If it does, then *ible* is the proper spelling. Example: *Divide* can lead to *division* or *divisive,* so *ible* is the correct ending.

This exercise of trying to discover spelling rules leads to rather high level linguistic understanding. It builds thinking skill, since it teaches where rules come from and what their limitations are. And it will solve some of your spelling problems.

But nothing will solve all spelling problems in English, contrary to the phonics hype extant in the homeschooling movement. The reading argument should not promise that wide reading produces naturally good spelling; it should only promise that it helps spelling. It builds a foundation of familiarity with words, which leads to the number one spelling skill, which is to know when a word might be wrong and needs to be checked. Second in importance is the desire to spell well, and your son evidently has that.

Don't set impossible goals. While spelling champion types enjoy learning thousands of words, the rest of us decide at some point that dictionaries can substitute for some of that mastery. Your son should realize that editors and others who work a lot with words always have dictionaries nearby.

On the other hand, don't give up too early. Keep plugging away with the various approaches you like, and in another year or two you will again see how much your son has improved.

Q. My fifth grade son cannot spell, yet he reads without formal phonics instruction. I just read aloud to my children and they began reading by themselves. I didn't think I needed phonics. Now I'm worried about this poor speller. Do I go back to phonics?

A. I can't clearly say whether or not it would help your son to go through a phonics book at this time. Probably he wouldn't mind it if he could zip through easy parts at his own pace, and he might pick up a few useful spelling helps on the way. Your son already knows a lot of phonics; he learned it on his own.

As I've said many times, phonics alone cannot make someone a good speller. Here are more illustrations. Let's say that your son wants to spell a word with long *a* sound in it and you say, "Well, just sound it out." If he knows phonics he then has a choice of *ay, ey, ai, aigh, ei* as in *eight*, *ea* as in *great*, or *a* with silent *e*.

Long *o* and *u* also have seven spellings each, while long *e* and *i* have eight spellings each. Short vowel sounds also run as high as seven spellings. Even consonants have multiple spellings. *T*, for instance, has six spellings. One of them is the *ed* ending as in the word *stepped*. On this word it is more helpful to know the grammar rule about *ed* ending for past tense than to know all the spellings for *t* sound.

Other knowledge about the language helps, too, and all this grows gradually with experience and immersion in language.

Q. I have girls 15, 17, and 18 years old who are all

good readers. In fact, they love to read, so I can't understand why they find it so difficult to spell. Words with five, six or seven letters create great anxiety, let alone larger words. Spelling is no problem for me, therefore, the situation is frustrating. What did they miss? How can I help them? How can I keep this from happening with our younger three? I have posters with the spelling rules on the wall. Any suggestions?

A. Because of your daughters' ages and reading ability, it doesn't seem likely that they have learning problems. So my best guess is that a dose of old fashioned hard work will help. With teenagers, I have seen the dictation method work wonders in just a few months time. Try dictating on Monday a paragraph from a beloved book. Then during the week find and analyze and study the spelling errors, and take more practice dictations, aiming for perfect spelling by Friday's dictation. You can refer to the poster rules as they apply to these words. Make your own family system for what to do if Friday's test is not quite perfect. One idea is to collect the troublesome words for special study later—if they are common enough to be useful. Another option is to continue with the same paragraph for another day or two until those words are mastered.

Try not to do mindless study like copying a word five times. Instead, encourage thinking and talking about why a word is spelled the way it is, why the student missed it, and how she will remember it next time.

After this spelling-in-context becomes

easier, the girls could spend a little time looking through a younger child's phonics book to find items they didn't learn or have forgotten. Study and practice those. Later, try more advanced word study books such as those which teach Greek and Latin roots and prefixes of English words.

For the younger children, too, it helps to use dictation and other attention to spelling in context. During primary years you could overlook some invented spelling in order to encourage more fluent writing. Then by fourth grade level you can be more insistent that the spelling be accurate, at least by the final draft of a writing assignment.

In the end, don't expect 100% perfection. We all need dictionaries at hand, except perhaps spelling champions who spend their lives mastering English spelling. The most helpful skill is to know when a word may be wrong and needs to be checked on.

Q. Is it important to keep reviewing or using a spelling program in junior and senior high grades?

A. It is important to continue working on spelling; that is a lifelong task. But as for a textbook-like program, you can see my feeling on some other answers in this chapter. If you use a book at all, use an all-in-one book rather than a grade by grade series. One example is *The Natural Speller* by Kathryn Stout. Another useful book would be one on Greek and Latin roots and prefixes.

Find ways to integrate spelling with all

other subjects. For instance, when you start a new course, from algebra to zoology, you could check the book glossary or index to find words new to your student. Begin learning the most common and important of these. This word learning will then be reinforced in context throughout the study of that course. Notice patterns such as the *centi* and *mil* prefixes in a math book or the *ium* noun ending in a chemistry book.

Also have the student collect common words which he misspells in his writing. Study of those will involve reviewing any spelling book rule which your student has forgotten. These in-context spelling ideas help build life-long habits of attention to spelling and, besides, they are more efficient than most spelling courses where words are studied in isolation from their context.

6.
Writing

Creative Ways To
Think about Writing

When you need to, you will find a way to communicate. As babies, your children gained the ability, over time, to let you know what they were thinking. The ability to talk was the beginning of their dialogue with the world around them.

There is a natural process to acquiring the skills of speaking and understanding. There is a similar process for learning to read the printed word, and yes, even learning to write. Success comes in many forms. As a 3- and 4-year-old, my daughter loved to sit and copy the letters she saw on book covers. Today she will read a story and write one that is similar in style, but original in content. For her, she began writing at that early age and hasn't stopped. When my 14-year-old son manages to write what he knows about a topic like plant cells, I am gratified. While never perfect, they have made great strides as communicators.

In this chapter, Ruth explains writing in understandable terms. She again takes the approach of demystifying that which unnerves us, and helps the whole process become more inviting. Whether your child was born to write, or is a pencil-phobic, you'll find ideas in this chapter that will help you think more creatively about writing.

—*Debbie*

Q. What suggestions do you have for language arts for a 6-year-old?

A. If we hadn't invented academic jargon like "language arts," people probably wouldn't be asking questions like this when their children turn 6. You have done an excellent job of teaching your child all the language knowledge and skills he knows so far, and that is quite a lot. From ground zero he has grown to be a competent speaker, with a large vocabulary for conversing on many topics, with good sentence construction ability, with correct grammar on practically all matters, and with ability to understand vocabulary and sentences more advanced than what he produces himself. In addition to all that oral language, your 6-year-old probably can write at least some letters and some words, including his name.

When you think of this amazing accomplishment with so young a child, a good question is why should you do anything much different in the next few years than you did in the first six. Continue to read together, converse together, learn about real people and things and events that you meet in everyday life. Begin to add some writing and reading gradually, just as you did with oral language. Formal curriculum is not necessary.

But my editor here is co-author of the Blue Book (first grade level) of the series *Learning Language Arts through Literature*. So I should mention that. Also, I have written *The Three R's*, which includes a writing manual and a reading manual for parents covering ages about 5 to 8. These are two items you might look at for teaching your 6-year-old.

Q. I have a wonderful boy of 9 who quit writing once he figured out (on his own) that there's a right and wrong way to spell. He also really struggles with handwriting because his mind works faster than his fingers. His art skill tells me it's not a fine motor skill problem. What do you suggest?

A. Try separating penmanship from writing in its larger sense. In fact, you could separate other parts of the total language task also. This could be a case of overload, wherein we expect young children to have correct letter forms, penmanship, spelling, sentence structure, grammar, punctuation, capitalization, and on and on, all while putting wonderful creative thoughts down on paper.

For a penmanship lesson, work on certain letter forms that your son needs improvement on. Or work on getting a uniform slant, or uniform height, or any one feature. For each lesson choose single words or a short phrase or sentence, perhaps from a memory verse. Write a model at the top of the sheet he will write on. Then there's no problem with spelling or anything extra; he can concentrate on making beautiful writing.

For writing an original story or informal paragraph, you could write or type as he dictates to you. You can put in the proper spelling, as well as punctuation and other mechanical features, and use his own words as much as possible. If something needs correcting you could sometimes discuss it with him on the spot and type it correctly, or you could wait until the editing stage, when either he will realize it doesn't sound correct or you could point it out and help him correct it.

What follows depends on the purpose of the piece. You may re-type for a final corrected copy, or he may learn keyboard skills and type it himself. Sometimes you don't need to re-do it, and once in a while he may need to make a nice handwritten copy. But don't turn every assignment into a penmanship marathon.

He will gradually gain confidence in spelling as he works on writing at these several skill levels: copying, writing from dictation, sometimes with pre-study of the sentences and sometimes without; and writing original compositions, sometimes dictating to you and sometimes writing or keyboarding them himself.

Q. My third grade son reads very well, spells well but dislikes written assignments of nearly every kind. I think the ability to write well is important. What is your recommendation as far as written assignments?

A. I agree that writing well is important. Or,

lacking that, speaking well. To lead or influence at every level of society, one needs good communication skills.

I will summarize here some ideas that are treated more fully in other questions. First, about half of all children seem to love writing and the other half dislike it. I check this repeatedly by asking the question in workshops. So you have many parents with you in this particular struggle.

If you're asking mostly about the penmanship level of writing, which many boys have trouble with at young ages, then require less writing. Let him answer questions orally. Or accept short answers, not insisting on complete sentence answers. Complete sentence answers are not especially grammatical English, anyway.

If you're asking about the communication level of writing, that is a longer teaching problem. I think we complicate it by using the term "creative writing," because then we think a sort of magic should happen in the brain to produce original thoughts on paper. But put something in the brain first. After your child experiences something or reads something, then you can help him develop his thoughts by conversing with him. After that preparation, he should find it easier to write it down.

It helps, also, to have an audience for the writing, or a real life purpose. After Christmas thank-you letters and reports to grandma about your family life are real. The latest idea I heard was writing to a sports idol to ask for a picture or an autograph. Collecting a story this month for the progress folder (portfolio) is half-real, half-school. Between the real writings, you'll have to require other writing, too. For the child who dislikes writing, try the dictation method described in the next answer (and in the high school chapter). With this method, the child does not need to produce his own thoughts, nevertheless he will learn the mechanics of writing and will grow in his feel for good sentences. Then when he does have something in his head to write, he will be better prepared with the skills to do so.

Q. I know that you recommend using the dictation method to teach writing skills. But my children, 6, 8 and 9, think it's hard. Should I make them do it anyway?

A. Within the dictation method as I worked it out, there is any level of difficulty that you need. The first level is simply copying, and a child can copy one word—his own name, for instance. Or even before that, he could trace over his name that you have written for him. So for children as old as yours you could find a level that's not too hard.

You can write out a model, perhaps a portion of a Bible verse: "Be kind" or "Be kind to one another." Over time, make the models longer, to match the children's ability. Later the models can come from books; you don't have to handwrite them yourself.

Besides copying, other levels of writing are: 1) to study the model and then write it from dictation, and 2) to write from dictation without seeing the model first.

There are levels of study, too. The earliest is just to learn the letter forms. Then learn how and why punctuation is used in the model passage, learn how the words are spelled, and how and why the sentences are formed as they are.

Stay with one particular model for several days or longer until the children reach the level of being able to write it from dictation without mistakes.

All this study can lead up to Benjamin Franklin's level, which is beyond dictation. He used to outline good articles from a British paper called "The Spectator." He put the outline away for a few days, and then he looked at the outline again and tried to rewrite the article from it. He said that he was sometimes gratified to feel that he had improved on the original.

All these variations and levels are within the dictation method. One main advantage of this method is that your children will be studying language whole. There are no blanks to fill in with *is* or *are*, no list of sentences to choose to end with periods or question marks, and so on. If we constantly break language into little bits for teaching, the bits do not add up to the whole.

While children are learning the basic mechanics of writing, you can use this method regularly—that is, almost every day except for days when they want to compose their own writing, and for other changes of pace. But when children can write two or three paragraphs of their own with good mechanics, then use this method only occasionally, mixed among other kinds of writing.

I should explain here that mechanics refers to the skills needed for writing rather than speaking. That includes spelling, punctuation, capitalization, indentation, centering titles and other formatting details. You can include penmanship at some levels, but there is no law against using word processing for these exercises.

Q. I have heard a lot about journaling being a good way to become a better writer, yet my children really don't like it. The agony we go through to fill up one page in a journal doesn't seem worth it. Should I continue to require them to write in their journals daily?

A. In any seminar audience if I ask for a show of hands, we find that roughly half of children like writing journals and half don't. I would be among the half that doesn't, so don't despair. Though I have never kept a diary for more than two days, I nevertheless grew up to write many books. I think this difference among children is related to psychological matters rather than to language matters.

So if your children don't like journal writing, I would say don't require it. You have a more difficult job than the journal moms, but you have to find other ways to get your children to write. Try real life ways, such as letters, and try one of the writing curriculums. I repeat here what I have said numerous times, that I recommend the books produced by homeschooling families above those made for classrooms.

Writing something original all the time is difficult. So for some children you can fall back often on the dictation method (described in another answer). This keeps their writing skills developing so that they will be ready when they do have something of their own to write.

Q. What is your opinion of the method called the writing process? My children hate to edit and revise and rewite their papers.

A. As with all formulaic systems, there is a limit to what it can accomplish. This system is not the whole of writing, nor the way all writers work. Revising works best when a piece is quite good already and just needs a bit of polishing. In worse cases, starting over fresh is a better answer. And in worst cases, forget it.

There should be a reason for reworking a piece of writing—preparing it for reading aloud, or preparing it to go into the progress folder to look at later. Here are a few of the kinds of changes your student can make when he does try revising: use better verbs, change passive to active, move phrases or clauses for better order, relocate whole thoughts for better order, delete irrelevant parts, add illustrations or more explanation to emphasize important points. Any and all ideas your student has learned about writing can be on his checklist to use during revision.

In the early days of word processing, some educators who specialized in writing, developed software to use for teaching students how to write. It was widely advertised and made a splash at first, but is now defunct. So much for educators teaching you how to write. I own this software and never use its features for outlining, organizing my notes and such. A lawyer uses it for organizing evidence for his cases. Some novelists outline their stories in detail; others start with their characters and don't know what will happen in the book.

So, I think each system you try will add something to your children's writing skills. But nowhere can you find *the* formula for writing.

Q. How much do you think I should focus on penmanship? Now that my first child is older (10) and still having difficulty writing neatly, my tendency is to push all the harder with my younger children. What is a good type of handwriting instruction and when should you begin to require handwriting practice?

A. I think we all have a tendency to overdo penmanship. Maybe that opinion goes back to my own school days when we had penmanship practice every day for years of our lives. I can't see that it was necessary at all. I learned the letter forms, I learned to slant uniformly, and I had trouble making a nice capital *E*. For all the elementary school years I simply repeated what I learned in first grade (they didn't use manuscript then), and my capital *E* problem continues to this day.

When children are first learning manuscript writing, you need lessons on the letter forms and uniformity of size, slant and spacing. After that, daily practice doesn't need to be called penmanship. Children can just write Bible verses or other content, where penmanship is secondary to whatever else you want to teach.

After they are fluent with manuscript writing, you can introduce cursive writing, and it's time for penmanship lessons again. The change should take about three weeks. If it doesn't go easily, then back off and continue manuscript for a few more months. There is absolutely no advantage in being early with cursive. It doesn't make the children smarter or make their education proceed at a more advanced level or anything like that. When they are adults, or even sixth graders, who's going to know or care when they made the change from manuscript to cursive?

After those initial lessons on penmanship, you may want to focus on it again from time to time as you see the need. Also use ongoing helps like posting a model alphabet on the wall and referring to it when your children are careless with certain letters.

For your older child, a crash course of some kind may help. Once in an open school with about one hundred third graders, we teachers decided to sort the children for a period by handwriting ability. I said, "I'll take the lowest ones." I think I was always a curriculum person first and a teacher second. I wanted to see if I could invent a way to help the poorest handwriters. That's when I developed what I called the head method that I describe in *You CAN Teach Your Child Successfully.*

Briefly, I obtained a model sentence from each child. Then I had individual conferences to point out something for improvement. Some items were to close *a*'s and *o*'s, to cross *t*'s more neatly, to make better loops in *l*'s or *e*'s, to make uniform height or uniform slant, to make straighter downstrokes on *g*'s and other descenders, or to correct the form of any particular letter. At first these children had numerous items needing improvement but I focused on just one or at most two. Then they rewrote the words with those items in them, or if their problem was slant, they could rewrite the whole sentence once or twice. Not too many repetitions, because the idea here is to get concentration instead of mindless repetition.

We continued in this manner, starting fresh with new sentences when we needed to. The papers were saved in each child's folder so they could see their own progress, and that was highly motivating.

The problems rapidly diminished. After a few days one father told his daughter, "Now you won't need to go to summer school." Penmanship, like spelling, is highly visible and a means by which people judge the quality of education. After three weeks there weren't enough problems to continue the system. I can't say that everybody had beautiful, artistic writing like some of the girls in Mrs. Hanson's group, but everybody had perfectly legible writing, and much improved artistic quality.

You might be interested in where I got the sentences. I called them the sayings of Solomon and they were proverbs about the value of learning. One unchurched boy told me that his family got out a Bible and read more sayings of Solomon.

The other crash course in *You CAN Teach* is called the rhythm method. I invented it in a one room school on Afognak Island so all ages could practice together. Three weeks of that also brought remarkable results. So from my experience, I recommend that you don't bore the children with forever penmanship practice. There are better ways to use the time.

Q. In comparison to the large amounts of written work required at schools, I am always worried that my children will not get enough practice in writing and will not be able to write as well as their peers. How much written work do you think an elementary student should do per day, or per week? Also, can you give some milestones on when most children can write a sentence, paragraph, page and report? I never know if they are ahead, behind or keeping up.

A. I am not up on how much written work schools now require. I do know that with today's political pressures for better results they send more and more homework, so that in itself means more writing. They believe in homework because research shows that more learning happens this way. As I analyze it, they are believing that a little homeschooling helps a little so more homeschooling will help more. They don't say it that way, of course.

I have met parents who realized they were spending hours per day homeschooling their children, so they decided they might as well quit school altogether. That makes wonderful sense. So I say don't use the schools as a model for how to develop writing.

I do suggest trying to produce some writing every day. This doesn't always have to be a "writing" lesson; sometimes it can be a history or science lesson, instead, that involves writing. One mother complained to me that they had spent most of a week writing Thank You's for Christmas presents, and that, along with making baked goods for elderly neighbors, didn't leave any time for schooling. Strange, how some people fall into real-life learning without even realizing it.

Why do I say every day? Because writing and speaking are two major ways that people influence society. All our learning is locked in our own minds if we can't communicate with others. Naturally there are exceptions; artists and inventors, for instance, can help and influence their world in other ways. But the day of the lone inventor may be past, and even the inventor must be able to communicate well with the people in his company who are planning next year's budget.

Every day, of course, means almost every day. If the baking and visiting take up some days, at least the children are growing in communication skills which will show up later in their writing.

As for how much writing, I'd say the quantity is not the main factor. College professors all groan inwardly when they explain a particular assignment and the first question is, "How many pages should it be?"

The age for writing a sentence is not an important milestone, because at that early level children have oral language abilities that far outstrip their writing abilities. During this stage, sometimes you'll be taking dictation from the children, and they'll be "writing" sentences before they are even school age. At first grade level, or whenever they learn to write the letters, children can quickly learn to capitalize the first letter and put a period at the end, and if you tolerate invented spelling, they can write a sentence as soon as they learn most of the letter forms and sounds.

This early writing depends on learning the mechanics. It will always lag behind children's thinking and composing level.

Later, children's writing more closely parallels the logic and thinking levels they have attained. Brief descriptions of average levels are included in another answer.

So your problem about keeping up becomes one of deciding whether a particular child could do better. Try helping one by what I call the meaning method. You could say, "When I read this, I'd like to know more about how you boys got the stuff up into the tree and how you put it together. It sounds too easy here. You just built the treehouse and I don't have much idea of all your hard work." Or say the child wrote this sentence. "You would not be afraid to ask because you know them better than other people." Your conversation might go something like this.

"Who is *them*?"

"Parents."

"Well, why don't you put that in so people can be sure who you mean?"

That's the meaning approach, and most everything can be fixed that way, especially through the elementary and into the junior high years. The grammar approach would be to say, "This pronoun has no antecedent," and let the child fix it on that basis.

You didn't say how old your children are, but my general advice is to save most grammar until the children are already good writers, maybe about junior high age. Until then, get them to write almost daily and use the meaning approach to help them improve.

Q. As you have given reading stages, can you tell about stages for grammar and composition?

A. For grammar, I'd keep it simple with just two stages. Up to about grade six or seven is the **intuitive stage**. After that, come the **abstract-analytical stages**. The intuitive stage is when the child picks up grammar knowledge intuitively, through normal language activities of conversing, reading, listening. We all learn about 99% of our grammar this way, and the grammar most of us use is about 99% correct. So during this stage, you're better off with no formal grammar teaching, just plenty of language activities. At about junior high level, you can begin formal study of grammar. Students can understand it then, after they write well. This won't improve their writing or speaking much, but it helps educate them about language.

I use grammar here in it's strict meaning of the study of the forms and structure of words, phrases and sentences. I do not include the mechanics of writing, which I have explained in other answers.

Composition ability grows along with general language and thinking ability. I gave writing samples and descriptions of stages in *You CAN Teach Your Child Successfully*, but I haven't named them. I'll try to do that here.

Encoding Stage. On average, this will be during the primary grades, and it corresponds with the decoding stage of reading. In this stage, children learn to form letters, leave spaces between words, capitalize, punctuate, and other basic mechanics and skills of writing.

Listing Stage. In fourth and fifth grades on average, children tend to list information without relating items well. Their stories tell happenings chronologically; their descriptions list objects and attributes. Their opinion pieces may list one or two reasons in fourth grade and up to four reasons in fifth grade. They seldom support their reasons, often do not connect them clearly with the original opinion, and often get off the track entirely. Sometimes they attempt a closing summary sentence. In writing how-to instructions, they can get chronological order, but again lose clarity because of insufficient relating. These children are becoming aware of an audience or reader, and they can direct their words to that audience.

Formal Stage. At sixth grade, average children are entering the formal stage, where written language is distinguished from spoken language by certain formalities such as introductory statements, good organization and summary sentences. Children have a better grasp of the wholeness and cohesiveness of a story or argument, even though some details do not yet cohere or are omitted. They can better relate ideas as to cause and effect, order of importance, psychological motivation, and so on. Because of better relating, their sentences grow more complex and varied.

Consolidation Stage. During junior high years there is slow growth in writing quality. These are years of physical growth spurt and brain growth spurt, and it seems that those are enough to handle at once. Students may need this time for consolidation and practice of existing writing skills, and when the time is right they move faster again.

Advanced Formal Stage. The rest of life can bring continual improvement in communicating with an audience through writing. As thinking grows, so grows the writing—with richer content, better organization, more creativity. By the end of high school, students, especially college bound ones, should have skills adequate to accomplish almost any adult writing task that life requires of them.

7.
Math

Math that Makes You Think

Help for Math Problems

When I was in school, I always felt like math was some mysterious process that you did that provided you with a correct answer. As a child, I wasn't always sure what that process was, so math became an extremely frustrating experience for me.

As a teacher, I was fortunate enough to have a professor in one of my education courses who said the same thing. She then proceeded to tell us about teaching a child to think mathematically. At that time (20 years ago), she introduced a concept that was radical to me, the use of manipulatives. The goal of any teacher of math is for the children not just to get the right answer, but to understand why it's right. I was thrilled! I felt like not only could the children understand math, maybe I would now too.

When I became a homeschooler, and started to teach math to my own children, I had the same concerns. I wanted my children to be able to do math, but more importantly, I wanted them to understand math. The pressure I felt as a child was now translated into the pressure of a math-challenged mom trying to make sure her children understood, and then were able to perform. As I searched for materials that would accomplish this goal, I have to say I became discouraged. The emphasis in homeschooling was on math performance, not math understanding. I started to worry again.

Shortly after starting our homeschooling, I came across Ruth's books, *The Three R's*. What an experience! She emphasized math understanding and she went about teaching math in such a way that even I could understand. I was so grateful to find Ruth's writings on the teaching of math. I have witnessed Ruth's help to families struggling with math. Once again, she takes the mystery out of the mysterious, and gives practical help. Out of that basis of peace, children can once again learn to think mathematically. If you need any help teaching elementary math, don't miss this chapter. You'll never look at math instruction the same way again.

—Debbie

Q. With regard to basic elements of math (patterns, classifying, sorting) how do you know when a child's "got it" and can move along to the next level. That is, how much repetition of what they can do is necessary?

A. There is no definite time when a child's got it for good and completely, but at some point you must move on anyway. We would like for learning to be linear so we can guide our children neatly along a line, through a path or up some steps and know when we are finished. In arithmetic more than anywhere else we cling to that idea. But even in arithmetic, children's learning is not linear. Later lessons on something else will enlarge your child's understanding of what you're trying to teach now. Each topic can be viewed from multiple sides.

Sudden spurts of understanding come along that may facilitate later learnings and strengthen past lessons all at once. The child is still growing in mental ability. And innumerable other factors affect the complex process of learning, so that the lines we try to lay out in our curriculums never work neatly. They just sort of work. So we should just sort of follow them.

Q. Do you have an idea how we should teach the times tables?

A. I think it's important to work by the principle of building understanding, rather than using rote memory only. Within this principle you can operate with any number of activities. Usually they will involve manipulatives, at least for a time.

To illustrate, I'll tell about a class I taught. I gave them all counters, which in our case were colorful, coin-shaped game chips. Then I demonstrated how to figure problems with the counters. For instance, for 2 X 8 the children made two piles of eight and counted them all to obtain the answer 16. After a few such problems they could proceed on their own working problems from their books.

After a time I suggested that they could write some answers on a sheet and refer to the sheet instead of counting repeatedly. So they wrote, for instance $2 \times 8 = 16$, and looked at their paper each time they needed that answer. They were happy to "cheat" like this and do their problems faster, but of course the sheets soon became a cumbersome jumble. Also, of course, they were memorizing some facts and didn't need either counters or sheets for those.

One day I showed a boy how he could make a row with all the answers for 2 times something. We numbered from 1 to 10 across his paper, put 2 at the left below them and then put each answer under its number. He was excited at the great shortcut, so I said, "You could make a row for 3s under that, and then 4s, and keep going if you want." He ran to his seat and filled out a whole chart of times tables, using his counters when he needed them. Then he bounced around the room excitedly showing other children how it worked.

Soon everyone had made a chart and were not using counters anymore. By then they also had memorized a lot of facts, and we could talk about how it was faster to do problems with the facts in their heads instead of referring to their charts. That's when we began memorizing the facts they still needed to learn.

At this point the job is not overwhelming, because you can have flashcards or practice sheets with just the facts your child needs to learn. Even here, try to avoid simple rote memory. For instance, learn a new fact by relating it to a known fact. If the child knows what five 5s are, then figure from that what six 5s are, and so on. Work on a few facts at a time. Review and practice and review.

I hope this illustrates the principle of building meaning before working on memory. Children using this approach should understand when they are memorizing 6 X 7 = 42 that it would be six piles of 7.

Q. Is memorization of times tables important? What is a good method to teach them?

A. There is almost universal agreement among educators (and parents) that children should memorize the times tables and other basic arithmetic facts. The best approach is to first build a good foundation of understanding and visualizing before working on the memory. For one suggested method see the preceding answer.

Q. We've tried everything to teach our 9-year-old son his math facts and they just don't stick? What would you recommend?

A. This could be because he learned the facts by rote memory without good understanding or inner visualization of what happens with the numbers. I would guess that he has no trouble with 2 plus 2, or with 2 times 5. The difference between those and more difficult facts is that those are easy to visualize. So work at making the others easy, too. Play dominos. Count by twos, by fives, by other numbers. Count money by nickels, by dimes. Observe a dozen eggs. Count them by twos. How many in half the carton? In one-third? Use a number line or hundred chart with the activities suggested with them. Learn the doubles. Then learn the almost doubles: if 6 and 6 make 12, then what are 6 and 7? Learn that adding 9 to a number makes 1 less than adding 10 to the number.

After lots of such activities and visualization, your son won't need to "remember" the facts; he will see them in his head, or be able to figure them out. At that time he can sort out by flashcards or by tests which of the facts he can't answer quickly. Those few, then, he can memorize or think of ways to figure easily.

Q. I hope you can help me determine whether math speed drills are effective in helping children learn their math facts. My son enjoys working math problems when he can take his time and count the numbers. I would like for him to be able to memorize his math facts, so I give him a speed drill four or five times a week to practice. Will this repetition help him memorize them? I should mention that he really dislikes speed drills.

A. I have never quite made up my mind about how much importance to attach to speed drills in math. Sometimes I think we value speed because children will score better on timed achievement tests or because it seems more virtuous than depending on calculators.

But your question is specifically about the effectiveness of speed drills in learning math facts. On this point, I think drills can be a little help at the right time. If your son enjoys counting out the numbers, I would guess that he is in the mental image stage of thinking about the math facts. That is, he needs to see in his head what is happening in the problems. I would not hurry him through this stage, but let him have lots of experience with the visualizing. This way he builds understanding of the facts he will later memorize. Later on, he should appreciate having a faster way to do his problems and may be more willing to do speed drills or games to gain that proficiency.

The repetition itself does not automatically help memorizing much, especially if you have too long a page of problems to do. To learn the times table of 3s, for instance, your son could drill just on that. If you're using flashcards you could put into a separate pile the ones that slow him down. Then he could work on those with his mind, not just with repetition. He could visualize that if five 3s are 15, then six 3s are 3 more, or 18. Or whatever helps the understanding. Then he can do the drill again and see his improvement.

If you can guide him in this kind of learning, which speeds up his time on a drill, you may find the drills become more motivating for him. But if he never likes the speed drills, I don't think it's any great loss. You can, instead, just require the memory of certain facts over the next couple of years and have him demonstrate his mastery at some minimum speed.

Q. *How do you motivate an 11-year-old boy to do math problems?*

A. With the question asked as it is, I'm going to assume that the boy does other studies without resisting and it's primarily on math problems where there is some sort of trouble. If the problems are rows of drill on essentially one kind of operation, you could say that if he gets all correct on the first row he doesn't have to do the next row, or the rest of the page. Or say that if he doesn't miss more than one on the first row he gets the reward. Adjust the requirement and the reward so that it works for your particular student.

This system helps to elicit high concentration and effort on the required problems in order to gain the reward of skipping other problems. Also, it makes good sense not to require excess drill on problems the child already can do.

Now, there may be something else here besides just boredom with drill. Maybe the child lacks some of the knowledge and skills needed to work the assignments. At age 10, or fifth grade, we might assume that children have mastered the four basic operations of arithmetic, but in many cases they don't have good understanding of these. In such a case, you need to slow down, use games and manipulatives, and gain understanding of the problems. It's better to discuss and understood two problems than to work twenty problems in a rote, drill fashion.

If these are story problems and your text

requires that the child write his operations, then the situation is different again. Some children can visualize and understand story problems. Their minds leap around and they arrive at an answer. But then we require that they retrace this leaping and write out the procedure in our society's formalized algorithm. I think this is a flaw in much of our math curriculum today. We spend too much time at young ages learning abstract, arbitrary forms, when these could be learned easily and quickly at a later age. (See more on this topic in a later answer.)

So, with story problems, you may sometimes just let the child write his answer and not the whole procedure. Other times, use discussion, drawings, manipulatives and any technique that helps to build understanding. Teach that there is more than one way to write or to work a problem, not just the one textbook way.

Q. It has become apparent to me that in upper elementary math the difference between A and B performance is primarily a matter of carefulness and not conceptual understanding nor even accuracy in calculations. The miscopied number, misread signs, faulty regrouping due to poorly aligned columns, missing units of measure, and carelessly read questions often account for ten of the deducted percentage points.

"Check your work" simply means "rework the whole assignment or test" to my children, and when they do they catch few of their errors and occasionally change correct answers. And so we go on in our coursework without truly remediating our shortcoming.

I would be delighted to hear from you that carefulness grows on a child with age. But not being so optimistic I must ask: Are there some guiding principles in proofing (not just reworking)? And how can we develop an attitude of carefulness from the start so that proofing might become less critical?

A. I don't know any quick fix for this common and continuing problem. But here are some suggestions that should help. First, teach about estimating. Discuss a problem and decide roughly what the answer will be. Even deciding whether it will be in the hundreds or in the thousands is helpful at first. Then calculate, and if the result is not near the estimate, the student must look for his error. This catches some of the slip-ups you mention. And more importantly, it is good for improving thinking skills. Some math teachers say that estimating is the most useful math skill any child could learn.

Second, work a problem two alternate ways. This can be as simple as adding up and then adding down or adding the left hand column first. The calculator can be an alternate way. The student should rework until he obtains the same answer both ways. Also, remember the old fashioned method of working backward from your answer, such as adding the remainder and the subtrahend to obtain the sum, or minuend.

Besides teaching the above techniques, you can motivate by rewarding accuracy. In some books it works to tell the child that if he gets all (or all but 1) correct on the first row he gets to skip the second row. Adjust this idea to suit your situation. Many homeschoolers have found it to be a powerful motivator.

I'll comment a bit on the *A* and *B* letter grades. If they haven't motivated your children to better accuracy, then that is just another evidence that grades don't fit homeshcooling. They were invented as a way for teachers to report to parents. Now, if you're the teacher reporting to some kind of umbrella school, something is backward if you can't revise the definitions to suit your teaching goals. Would you like to say something like *A* is 100% accuracy on the first row, and *B* is 100% accuracy on the second try—the second row?

For you and any readers who may be in this situation, particularly at elementary levels, you might try negotiating with the schools to be flexible where you need it. Homeschoolers earlier in the movement accomplished some good changes in this way.

Q. I really messed up somewhere. My daughter is in fifth grade and she can't do the story problems. When my husband asks her about a problem she can usually tell him what the answer is, but she still can't write it down anymore than she does for me.

A. I don't think the problem is with you; it is with our whole system of teaching arithmetic. I'd say just let your daughter write or tell you the answer and forget for now writing it down in the form the textbook may be requiring. Read on for my reasons (some of them).

When I wrote *An Easy Start in Arithmetic* in the early 1980s, I suggested not using arithmetic texts at all in first and second grades, and possibly in third grade, too, if parents felt comfortable with that. That suggestion was as much as I thought I could get away with in those days; no one would have listened at all if I had said what I really believed.

But times have changed, and now I probably can get away with saying that at least some families who are brave enough to try it can forego arithmetic texts for longer than that. I read about the child who "never saw an arithmetic text until fifth grade" or of the eighth grader who learned how to "write the problems down" just before he had to take an achievement test. And these students succeed. Many more are succeeding with the better textbooks produced by homeschooling families, which teach for understanding and not rule-learning.

Your experience with story problems is very common. What's happening is that your daughter can visualize the problem, and her mind leaps around and arrives at the answer. Then her text wants her to write down the solution in a certain adult-determined abstract algorithm. We'd have fewer struggles if we saved that abstract part until later. At the right time children can quickly and easily learn to write the problems. But the way we're doing it now, they spend years of arithmetic time learning exactly how adults want it written.

For a simple example, John Holt used a kindergarten arithmetic book as bedtime reading in a boarding school. Children who had not already learned that workbooks were hard could complete a whole book in just a night or two. Traditional kindergartens take a whole year of lessons to complete that work because they're spending so much time teaching exactly where to place the numbers and the plus signs and so on. Real arithmetic thinking suffers in the process.

Here's another example I will quote from "Home Education Magazine." It's part of an online discussion among homeschool moms.

> I got good grades in math...but I simply knew it and did it by the algorithms. I can't say I really had a good, intuitive grasp....I just followed the rules that they told me.

> I learned [this example] from my son during our first year of homeschooling: 5+7=? He promptly—and I mean promptly—answered 12. When I asked him how he had solved the problem so quickly (he was 7 at the time) he explained that 5+5=10, and 10+2=12. I had to ask him to explain it several times before I understood where he got the 5+5 (from breaking 7 into 5 and 2). I was stunned. I didn't know you could break numbers up like that.

This is so good that I have to quote another section of the conversation. It illustrates, I think, how your daughter can understand the real arithmetic in her problems, but not the artificial specific adult algorithm the text wants her to write.

> Or the time he turned a joke into a math lesson for mom: "What has 18 legs and

catches flies?" he (still only 7) asks. "I don't know," I reply. "A baseball team," he states. Mom, seizing that 'teachable moment' asks, "Well, then, can you tell me how many people are on that baseball team?" "Hmmm," he says, "let me think about this....No, don't help me...(silence for about 30 seconds)...9 people on the team." Mom, knowing we have not yet studied division, is stunned. "How did you figure that out?" "Well," he says, "I know that each person has 2 legs, and there are 5 twos in 10 and 4 twos in 8 and 5 and 4 is 9, so there's 9 people on the team."

That little boy had been learning from what the mom called a "conceptually based" arithmetic program. Your daughter appears to understand the arithmetic concepts, so you haven't messed up. You've taught what's most important. It's your book that's messed up.

8.
Bible

Learning from the Master Teacher

The Bible is considered the most important piece of literature that the world has known. To study it with your children is to acquaint them with a masterpiece. But to Christian homeschoolers, the study of the Bible comes with an added benefit—an introduction to the Master.

One Sunday afternoon when my son was about six, he brought his new favorite dinosaur book from the library out to the living room to read. Leafing through the pictures, he stopped and gave me a puzzled look. He had come upon a picture that was supposed to be what the first man looked like. He asked me if that was true. I looked at the picture and asked him what Bible verse we had been memorizing. He quickly rattled off Genesis 1:27, which says, "And God created man in his own image, in the image of God he created him; male and female he created them." I asked him if he thought that was what God looked like. He vigorously shook his head no. A look of amazement came over his face. "You mean not all books tell the truth?"

It was a moment I will never forget. God's Word had been my son's teacher in those few, electric minutes. He came up against the world's philosophy, measured it against God's Word, and found it lacking. I didn't have to prepare elaborate lessons or find a way to stuff this information in his head. The Word of God had been alive for him, teaching him a deep and penetrating lesson.

Ruth's vast scholarship in the area of the Bible is impressive, but even more impressive is the way she helps us make opportunities for the Living Word to speak to us and our children. Read on to find ways you can make Scripture the heart of your homeschooling life.

—Debbie

Q. What curriculum do you recommend to use for teaching Bible to my children? We have quite an age span (from elementary to high school) yet would like to do this part of our teaching with the children together.

A. I don't recommend specific curriculum for Bible, just as is my policy for other subjects. Especially in Bible, no full curriculum could do it justice. The Bible itself is the best core curriculum to use.

In a recent magazine where families were sharing what they do for Bible teaching, I was astounded at both the amount of Bible and the range of teaching approaches reported by these families, all the way from reading a few verses at the dinner table and talking about them to having the children write out their own copies of the Bible in a notebook. Homeschoolers are certainly obeying the command to teach God's words diligently, to talk of them when they sit in the house, and walk by the way and rise up. And they fill their doorposts and gates with Scripture reminders.

Families use oral reading at all levels, from listening up to practiced presentations as for a speech class. They use study at all levels. A few of their ideas are: studying and reading through a selected book repeatedly for a month; marking and coloring their Bibles according to a plan; copying portions (sometimes the whole Bible!) into a notebook; discussing or writing according to a plan (observations, applications, etc.); narrating the content after a family reading, beginning with the youngest child and ending with the eldest; writing about the content that was just discussed; keeping a devotional journal; and memorizing.

With the Bible as core, I would say that you and other families could have just as much variety in the related materials you choose. Reference books—atlases, concordances and such—are probably important for everybody, and if you're into computers, learn to use computer references as well.

Choose other books according to topics within various areas such as prophecy, creationism, history, systematic theology, family living, or whatever you may become interested in. Here I am referring to "real books," not curriculum items. Real books are by real authors (not committees) who have specialized in their particular area. By doing this over the years you will collect a fine library of Bible study books that will serve you well throughout life. Our family has tended to collect books especially on Genesis and Daniel. We borrow them from each other even today. Or someone calls from another state and asks what Philip Mauro said about a particular passage. Used workbooks from Sunday school or elsewhere don't share this honored place in our library. The fact is, they don't have any place at all for our grown family.

If you find curriculum items that you like, that teach something you want your children to learn, use them for a time. Call them unit studies if you want. This is simply adding variety to your core of the Bible.

Q. When do you suggest that we start teaching our children to do formal Bible study (looking up word meanings, using concordances, etc.)? I am uncertain about this, so I just haven't tried it. Also, when I look at most Bible curriculum, it seems so dry that I don't think my children will find it interesting. I want their study of the Bible to be disciplined, yet enjoyable. I know it sounds like I'm asking the impossible, but do you have any suggestions?

A. The concordance question first: I'd say just loosen up; don't be formal about Bible study. If you have family Bible reading and discussion time, questions will arise when a concordance or Bible dictionary or atlas will hold the answer. At first, while your children are young, you can get the book and find the answer. Let them see you valuing these references. After your oldest child has learned about alphabetizing and can find words in a dictionary, send that child for the concordance, and gradually your children will be introduced to these valuable helps. Along the way you can teach more about the Strong's numbers, about map reading, using various indexes, and such. Teach these one by one as occasion arises or have a couple of formal lessons if that seems needed.

Now the curriculum question: I agree with your assessment of most Bible curriculums. Having spent thirteen years in that work myself, I could give lots of reasons why you don't often find higher quality, but here I'll just say don't buy what you don't like. Read the preceding answer for ideas from homeschooling families.

Q. How important do you think memorizing Scripture is? It may sound silly, but my children really like having a chart with stars on it for each Scripture they memorize and can say at church. Do you think something like that would be good for our homeschool?

A. Stars may be old and familiar to us, but if they're new and exciting to your children, go ahead and use them. Sticking on the glistening stars is a pleasure in itself. But more important, is the fact that this is a record of achievement and progress for your children. I sometimes ask how long bowlers or golfers would continue bowling and golfing if they didn't keep score.

Not long, I think.

Now on the main question, I think memorizing Scripture is the best thing you can do in your homeschool. Our children all should grow up learning verses, longer passages, chapters and sometimes whole books from memory. Sunday school, VBS and clubs should all work on this, and you can strengthen that learning by reviewing the same verses at home. Review is important for retaining the verse over the long term, and too often Sunday schools just forget last week's verse and teach a new one this week.

It is useful to learn verses by categories, such as salvation, giving, what to speak about, what to think and meditate on, commands for families, and so forth. And it's helpful to learn by gimmicks, such as verses beginning with each letter of the alphabet. Some of the psalms were written according to the Hebrew alphabet so the people could more easily remember and sing the words to a long psalm. Numerous memory systems have been preplanned and you could use one of those or develop your own.

I would especially urge you to teach your children how to learn longer passages. This is best done not verse by verse but as a whole. You could start this as a family. Choose Psalm 23 or Psalm 100 or the Beatitudes or other favorite passage, and read it together every day. Each day you could work on a detail such as making sure the children pronounce a difficult word correctly or explaining what the shepherd does with his rod and staff. As time goes on, push the children to look up from their Bibles for as much of the recitation as they can. Try other ideas, for instance reciting in turns around the table with each person taking up where the previous one gets stuck. Or father reads an opening word or two and the rest of the family continues reciting for a verse or two. Then father prompts again. Always read or recite through the whole passage. Only when the passage is learned almost perfectly should you take extra time to focus on a difficult verse or section that seems to be holding up your mastery of the passage.

After you learn a passage, review it on what researchers call a "diminishing schedule." That is, at first you review it every day, then every week for a while, then perhaps once a month, then twice a year and then once a year. You can tell whether to schedule your review sessions more or less often by how well your children recite at a review session.

Older children who know this system of memorizing can, on their own, memorize longer chapters or whole favorite books of the Bible. What better preparation for life can you give your children than to know the Bible so familiarly as this? The main advantage is that it feeds their hearts. But the side effects are good too. The beautiful language and literary character of the Bible will increase their writing and speaking skills. The truth in the Bible will increase their logic and thinking skills. And the discipline of memorizing will help in all other learning.

Q. What do you think of children's Bible story books for our Bible curriculum? Our children are young (ages 6 and 8) and this seems to be what they get the most out of. They also love videos of Bible stories, and tapes. My husband and I pray together with the children each night, encouraging them to pray about their concerns, as well as us praying for them. Do you think this is adequate or should we have an official devotional, Bible curriculum time?

A. In another answer here I describe the wide variety of approaches homeschooling families use, and you fit well into that range. You didn't mention memorizing, but you probably do that, too, at least through Sunday school and VBS.

I will comment on Bible story books and tapes and videos. The quality of these varies, and often you will find inaccuracies. Sometimes make Bible study sessions out of evaluating how accurate these are. You could read the story directly from the Bible and help the children figure out how well their version matches the original. Also from time to time you might add some theology to the story. A particular story shows how powerful God is, or how much He hates sin or whatever. Your materials may already do this.

At primary ages, as your children are, Bible stories are ideal. This is the foundational content you will need to build upon when you later are trying to teach the Bible as history or as theology or anything else.

Q. When do you feel it is appropriate to go into depth teaching the history surrounding the Bible events, for example the Old Testament. Though my children are very familiar with Bible stories and events, they are not very familiar with the cultures or events surrounding these Scripture accounts. Should I wait and teach this as part of my son's high school coursework on ancient history? I must admit that I have thought of teaching it earlier, but it just seemed too complicated for my children to grasp.

A. You're right that that kind of history seems too complicated for elementary children, and much of it too complicated even for high school. I know a college history professor who says that we should begin studying history at age 26.

I fear that among homeschoolers, too many parents see history as black and white, as a simple account of what really happened. That is, they think it will be that way if only they can get the right books. But no history book except God's has an accurate analysis and account of what really happened.

This is not to despair, but this is to realize that history is one area where students can learn good thinking skills and study skills. They can compare book with book, or raise questions for family discussion. And, hopefully, some will raise questions that they will carry into their future careers and find answers for the rest of us. This is my fond hope for the homeschooling movement.

In the meantime, you can teach bits of culture or history. And make connections at any age where the children have the background. For instance, in the Bible story of the birth of Christ, you'll read of Caesar Augustus. If your children have read anything about the Roman Empire, you can make a few connections. Study a historical map and notice how the empire spread far and encompassed the land of Israel. In the story of Paul's travels, again connect with any city or area the children have previously studied. Focus on the most meaningful, maybe Athens and the Greeks. But explain that by the time of Christ and Paul, Greece was a part of the Roman empire. As for going into depth, you could pretty much do what you want about that. I'd just say that if you go into depth about everything, you'll get off the track of your main study, which is the Bible. As you suggest, you could do some of this in high school history, but there's too much to ever do it all.

Now the Old Testament is another story. You can connect geography more than history, I think. Teach where Egypt is in relation to Canaan, that Babylon and Persia are east (now known as Iraq and Iran), and that the Ararat Mountains are north. Mount Ararat, interestingly, on most Bible maps does not appear together on the same map with Canaan or with the Tigris and Euphrates Rivers. But if you can find a map extensive enough, then children can connect the Noah story and see where his descendents first traveled down to the area of the two rivers and learn that Abram grew up there before he went to Canaan.

Egypt and the other kingdoms had boundaries which expanded and contracted during early history, Egypt at times extending up to Canaan. Comparison of historical maps with modern maps will give children some idea that boundaries are not static. They need a general understanding of Joseph in Egypt, and of Jacob's whole family moving down there during a famine, and of the dramatic events later during Moses's and Joshua's time.

That's a general framework of earlier Old Testament history, and perhaps by the early teen years children can grasp the connectedness of it even if they couldn't pass a test on details. Later history includes the united kingdom under David and Solomon, the divided kingdom and then the captivity and return. To get a feel of connectedness, to get the big picture, I think some geography study from time to time will be as helpful as history.

The background of Bible stories that your children have is important. That's the information they will use to build up the picture. And after getting this big picture they can study in more depth the history of various empires or times or leaders or common people and fit those learnings into their places. But that's a major job. So don't get discouraged if it seems too much for the children to grasp. Do what you can and they'll be started on a lifetime of fascinating learning. You have a better goal than the curriculums and storybooks that focus mainly on Bible stories in disconnected fashion.

Now I want to add a bit about Egypt. Study of ancient Egypt seems to be a favorite among homeschoolers. But when you get into detail about individual pharaohs and their chronology, you can't at this time match things up with Moses and the Exodus and other Bible events. Many historians like it that way; they can say that the Exodus is a myth or that it was a small tribal migration that didn't affect Egypt much. But from the Bible story you can see that Egypt was devastated by that event. It took them a long time to recover, so that all through the period of the judges they never were among the enemies who attacked and plundered Israel.

I think the problem is that we have the wrong chronology for Egypt. And since the archeology and history of surrounding nations are tied to Egypt's, they all have major problems in their chronology too. Some scholars are now writing about this and saying that several centuries need to be dropped (actually overlapped with each other) in our usual Egyptian chronology.

With the new chronologies, the Exodus would come at the collapse of the middle kingdom of Egypt. Many other events also match up better with the Bible, and all of history back to the Tower of Babel is shortened. There will be no quick changeover to a new and better chronology because the royalties and reputations of professors and textbook writers are at stake. But I hope, if our world has enough time left to it, that you homeschoolers will raise some historians, archeologists, linguists of ancient languages, professors and others so that this picture can be straightened out.

All that is to say that if you study in depth the history surrounding the Bible, don't look for black and white, simple accounts of what really happened. Instead, expect to become involved in intriguing puzzles that lead you far deeper than you thought to go.

Q. *Do you suggest teaching the principles of Creation Science as a separate science course, or do you think I should just intermingle these ideas throughout our science learning? I thought we had pretty much done that, but then upon reading Henry Morris and Gary Parker's book,* What Is Creation Science?, *I found that they went into much greater depth than I had. It almost feels like I should make this a separate course for my high school aged son. What do you think?*

A. You could mix things any way you want. To avoid having too many subjects, you could study a book, like the one you mention, as a science unit and then return to your regular science course, if you have one. I am convinced that regular reading of the creationists' books and magazines should cover enough science topics for the general education of most students. So that's a good option. There definitely are too many falsehoods in secular textbooks to rely heavily on them. One teenage friend here told me that when his class came to the geological column in their book the teacher said, "You can believe this if you want to, but I don't."

This whole curriculum question will soon be moot, as a couple of creationist organizations are now producing science curriculums for homeschoolers. And other homeschooling people are publishing units and courses on science, using the creationist viewpoint.

I should add that a good grasp of the creation-evolution controversy is extremely important. Evolution in some form has always existed, ever since Satan said to Eve, "You will be as gods." That view has been destructive throughout history, and it's destroying society in our times, too. People must believe in a Creator God to whom they are answerable, before they see their need of a Savior.

Q. Why did you write Adam and His Kin *in narrative form as you did?*

A. I think I understand that behind this question is a concern for whether this form somehow tampers with the truth of Scripture, so I'll try to address this concern.

Part of the history of this book is that I had spent thirteen years writing Bible lessons. I had written about creation and the Flood and other early events a number of times for several different age levels, so it would have been fairly easy for me to write *Adam* as a straightforward account in the manner that a teacher might tell it to her class. And I, in fact, made several false starts on the book, trying out such forms. But they did not satisfy me. I knew they would not accomplish what I wanted to accomplish.

We all have had Sunday school lessons and heard sermons on the Flood. We have read the Bible and Bible story books and children's picture books. And yet I could hear a radio preacher explaining details about Noah building the ark near Mount Ararat. Now the Bible says that he *landed* on the mountains of Ararat, and my view is that we don't know where Noah lived before the Flood and whether those mountains even existed in his ark building time.

All the straightforward lessons have not led many people to think clearly about those geographical matters and, more importantly, such matters as the drastic changes that sin wrought in the earth and the far-reaching results of the catastrophe at Babel. Sunday school lessons, in fact, sometimes treated with light humor the idea of workmen one morning not understanding each other's speech.

So I hoped that my narrative approach would help people to see the events through new eyes, and help them to think more clearly and with renewed interest about our earliest history. I am gratified to see, through letters and comments, that this happened for many people.

I will also point out that preachers can make errors in their sermons while telling Bible events. Commentators can err in their commentaries. Lesson writers can err in their lessons. So, also, Bible story and picture book writers. All of these may add details or suppositions not in the succinct Bible accounts, in order to help their arguments or purposes. Shall I mention the Sunday school pictures which show Noah as a cave man with a wooden club in his hand?

Now I certainly have errors in my writing too. But I must risk my historical narrative effort, along with all the above efforts, and hope that it enriches some people's Bible study.

As a reading teacher, I will add another comment. People who are looking for only "true" books, with just the historical facts, without a biased viewpoint, with events "as they really happened," will not find them. The

Bible is the only completely dependable and true book. What we must do instead is to teach our children a higher level of reading and thinking so they are able to deal properly with various kinds of writing.

Q. How can you say that Adam and Noah wrote parts of Genesis when writing wasn't even invented in their time?

A. This question reveals our culture's brainwashing in history. These days, many of us have learned not to believe the evolutionary brainwashing in science, thanks to wonderful science writers and speakers. But we are less aware that the evolutionary pattern of thinking pervades history, too.

Whenever the history books tell of "developing" language or agriculture or town life or religions or anything else, they are teaching in evolution terms. They assume man started as a brute and gradually developed a civilized life.

But the Bible history is different. Adam knew the pure language and talked with God using that pure language that we, too, will use someday. Since Babel, languages have a pattern of gradually deteriorating rather than developing. Adam lived more than 900 years; he certainly could have made a writing system himself if he needed to—that is, if God didn't make it for him. I believe that the original writing system incorporated both the sound elements of alphabetic writing and the meaning elements of pictographic writing. I can't go into detail here, but recent research indicates this, and philosophically it fits the Bible view of history. Later writing systems, that came after Babel, were less perfect, incorporating only parts of the original perfect system.

Internal evidences in the Bible also show that Moses had ancient records to draw from, and I explain some of these in my book, *GENESIS: Finding Our Roots.* So I say, yes, Adam wrote about the garden of Eden, and Noah and his sons wrote about the Flood.

Further, I say that we must all work at eliminating evolutionary thinking from our history studies until we do as well as we have learned to do in science.

Q. If the Bible was our only book to teach from, would it be enough? Math, too?

A. Because of the math tag, I interpret this to mean, "Can we teach all the expected curriculum by using only the Bible," rather than meaning, "If we teach only the Bible, is that a good enough education?" To my second rendering here, some could develop a good argument for a yes answer, and others would counter with a dominion view that God wants us to learn how to till the ground and otherwise learn about and care for the earth He has given us, in addition to learning the Bible.

With my first rendering, we can see arguments for both sides also. Earlier generations often taught their children to read by using what was the only book in many homes, the Bible. But that presupposes that the parent had in her head some knowledge of the alphabet and letter sounds. (In those days they didn't use phonics as we know it.) That earlier mom could also teach writing and penmanship by using Bible passages, but that presupposes that she had in her head a knowledge of cursive letter forms. Now with math, I'm sure someone could invent any kind of problem for children to work, beginning with 2 plus 2 (Adam and Eve and their first two sons) on up to highly complex math. But again it presupposes that the teacher knows what math to teach.

So in today's world, it is more practical to have some books with cursive letter forms or math problems to make our teaching easier.

But this is a wonderful question to contemplate. Are we using too much non-Biblical stuff? Do some textbooks slip in worldly thinking unaware? I'd say yes. When our Christian students go off to universities and lose their faith in shockingly high numbers, then they are not grounded well enough in the Bible. They cannot give a reason for the faith that is in them. Not only science professors, but literature and history professors, are difficult for young Christian students to stand against. These show the Bible as myths. Psychology and philosophy professors, too, teach anti-Bible theories.

To meet all this, the student needs a good knowledge of the Bible and basic theology, and practice in comparing the world's theories with Bible truths. We need Bible in connection with every subject. What would we do if we asked this question: "If I have only one more year to teach my children, what would I teach them this year?"

9.
High School

Yes, Virginia, You *CAN* Homeschool Your High Schooler!

If ever there were any aspect of home-schooling life where we need God's peace, it is facing the challenges of homeschooling a high schooler. Ruth's first-ever discussion in print of teaching high schoolers is reassuring. She reminds us of the principles we believed and used for elementary grades and extends them out further, to the high school level. She gives us insight and advice on matters of testing and transcripts and curriculum, yet she helps us maintain our focus.

While I'd like to say that this is a one-time struggle, I'm afraid I can't. As with all other stands that we take while trying to follow the Lord's guidance, there have been times when I wanted to do one or all of the following with my high schooler:

1) enroll him in school,

2) enroll him in any credit-granting institu-
   tion I could find, no matter how much it

cost or how much paperwork it required,

3) obsess endlessly about whether or not I was covering every subject he might need to face in his school or life work.

You may choose to enroll your child in a school or other situation, but this is the answer only when you can do it in peace, not out of fear or frustration. There is something about the prospect of accepting the responsibility for high school that seems different from the earlier grades of homeschooling. Somehow committing to this seems scarier, but I must remind myself that I felt that way at one time about homeschooling my first grader. The challenge is new, but the provision is the same. As we are able to let the Lord lead us, He gives us His peace and He provides for our homeschooling high schoolers. I have seen Him do it for our family. I know He will do it for yours, too.

—Debbie

Q. What standard, or course of study do you recommend a high school student follow so that he will be prepared for college?

A. I will approach this question by looking at the result you want at the end of a high school career, rather than by listing building blocks to get there. In these days, you want the ability to score high enough on college entrance exams.

First and foremost the student needs a high level of reading ability. He must be able to read and understand a wide variety of materials, literary and scientific. If you realize that he doesn't need memorized science information, for example, for these tests, it can alter your way of teaching. He needs, instead, the vocabulary and understanding to read selections on various specialized branches of science so that he can answer questions based on each selection. Some questions will have answers specifically given in the selection and some will require thinking and inferring beyond the given information.

That high level of thinking is transferable among topics. In other words, if the student knows a lot of biology and can think critically in that subject, he can read about a less familiar subject, say botany or chemistry, and do well on many of those questions, too.

If the student can read like that in science, history, literature and other subjects, he should do very well on the verbal parts of the tests. And in math he needs a minimum of high school algebra and geometry to do well enough on the math parts. Some homeschoolers get those during the junior high years. If the student intends to go into engineering or similar fields, you should have math more than that.

Now, a student who can read and think as described above, should also be able to write near that level. His writing should show clarity of thinking and good organization, as well as command of spelling and the mechanics of writing.

When you view the outcomes in these general terms, you can see that it really doesn't matter whether your student happened to read about Alexander's conquests but not Napoleon's campaigns. It is impossible to study everything that a group of people would list as essential. Textbooks try to do that, but they sacrifice much depth and interest and thinking in order to skim over numerous topics.

So, to prepare for college entrance tests, you can work on reading and writing and general knowledge in a variety of fields, and on some math. In addition, your choice of college may have other requirements, such as foreign language. You'll have to find out what those are as early as possible and include them in your plans.

Q. You CAN Teach Your Child Successfully *for grades 4 to 8 is good, but what do you do after eighth grade?*

A. Many of the ideas in that book, especially for the content subjects, can carry right on over from eighth grade into high school, for instance the idea of learning history from real books instead of dull textbooks. So don't panic; there's no need to make drastic changes once your children reach high school age.

More and more people are now writing good books on the high school level. From those and from convention speakers you can learn of the variety of ideas for home learning and for branching out into apprenticeships or community college courses or elsewhere. Also you can learn from these about such matters as what to do about graduations, keeping records and getting into college. Wonderful pioneers in the homeschool movement have gone before.

Q. Some of my friends are so concerned about transcripts and record keeping that they buy piles of textbooks, and labor through all those just so they can put courses and grades on a transcript. It seems artificial and dull to me, and not the way I want my two children to experience their high school years. What is your view? Do we need to follow traditional high school courses?

A. I had fun exploring this question when I wrote my one-and-only fiction book, *The Cabin and the Ice Palace*. The children in Schuliland called their studies Reaching Out, Looking In, Making Over, Planning Ahead, and others. And I get quite excited when I see homeschoolers today experimenting along similar lines. Such originality and freshness is a large part of why I call homeschooling the healthiest movement in education today.

But you have certain hoops to jump through because of your state laws or college entrance requirements, so you have to be creative with those, too. Inge Cannon* suggests a system of jotting onto cards various activities, books read, projects done, trips or museum visits, papers written, etc., and when you get enough hours gathered on one card you can make a name for the course, English Composition I, or Medieval History, or whatever. Put Bible study onto a history or literature card. In other words, you do things your way, but you bend the records their way. Along with this freedom, you could combine some traditional courses. College bound students, for instance, usually work systematically on math courses.

I'd like to suggest a Schuliland combination of Bible and all the sciences. If you subscribe to the Australian "Creation" magazine** your high schooler and the whole family can learn from the articles and short items in it. Students will learn the evolution teachings of the schools but will practice advanced thinking skills by analyzing problems of evolution and comparing everything with Bible teachings. This magazine is colorful, well illustrated, contains pages for younger children, and is excellent in every way. I think every Christian student needs a few years of this education before going off to college, even to most of our Christian colleges today. And I have no doubt that they will score high enough on science in their achievement tests or college entrance exams.

*Inge Cannon's materials, such as Apprenticeship Plus are available from Education PLUS+.

**Available from Answers in Genesis, PO Box 6330, Florence KY 41022, 800-778-3390. Price as of this writing is $22 per year.

Q. We're looking at textbooks for my son's first year of high school, and I am getting depressed about homeschooling at this level. Time-wise it seems impossible to complete all the books and, besides, they would be a real killer of his interest and enthusiasm. Is there a way to teach this course-type material to make it livable, yet cover the basic information about each topic?

A. Reading behind the lines, I would guess that you have made it livable through the elementary grades. So carry your successful procedures and ideas into high school. You don't need to be a slave to textbooks in high school any more than you were in lower grades. Don't be intimidated by textbooks. Read what I said about them in the curriculum chapter.

With a lowered view of textbooks, you should find it easier to eliminate some books entirely and to use others as your common sense would lead you. English composition books can easily go if you work writing into science and other subjects. Some grammar study along the way would be appropriate, but don't use graded textbook series for this; use only one book, such as a college English handbook, through all the teen years. Literature texts could easily go, since literature is widely available in libraries and elsewhere. Videos and movies can help here, especially for students who are not voracious readers. Videos also help for languages. And any subject. Computers, too.

Science textbooks could easily go if you use the Bible and science suggestions that I mentioned in the preceding answer. For students serious about pursuing a science major, supplement this with some of the creation science books as well as the magazine. And, if you can, add textbook courses on chemistry and physics, the more mathematical of the sciences.

Debbie's Note: Science might be a good area to try to co-op in. Our homeschooling group and church have created a co-op with homeschool parents teaching or a homeschool friendly person who has expertise in areas where some of the moms may feel lacking, or don't have the equipment. It has worked well, and the kids and moms all seem to be enjoying the arrangement. We charge tuition and pay the teachers, so no one ends up feeling imposed on. My children have greatly enjoyed getting to see their homeschooling friends, and they like the classroom experience in limited amounts. The co-op has also helped meet the teens' need to get together, to have a group of friends to do things with after school.

To continue, history textbooks can easily go, and real books be substituted instead. You can use textbooks as frameworks, if you feel more comfortable that way. That is, you can look at the section on ancient Greece and get ideas for people and events to read about. Then after reading interesting books on Greece you could turn again to the textbook for a summary and wrap-up. Read through the section and see how the book organizes and relates events, and what it emphasizes as important, and so on. The textbook will be more meaningful with the background the student now has, and it may even be more interesting.

As for government, economics, and current events, you can handle them in any of the above ways, depending on how much you wish to emphasize them. A highly useful method for any topic, even for adults, is to find a good children's book on the topic. Children's writers are skilled at making complex topics clear and understandable, so that makes a good starting point for studying anything. In fact, for subjects that you only want an acquaintance with, this method can be the whole. Also on these subjects, which today include much that is controversial, you could discuss current writings and political speakers and such. You could subscribe to "WORLD" magazine,* which gives news viewed from a Biblical perspective. Or to "LINK-Homeschooler,"** a free publication which teaches about the plight of Christians in many nations of the world.

For music and other arts, work in what you can in your family. Attend live concerts and plays, as well as listen to some at home. Visit art museums or galleries, just a room or so at a time; don't overload. Do some music and art yourself, of any kind. Manual arts, agriculture, ranching, business, trades, computers, and any other conceivable learning—work these in according to your own family interests.

A further word about high school studies: you do not need to follow semester patterns, studying several subjects at a time. Sometimes you may immerse yourself in only one subject for three weeks and then change pace to another pattern. Some subjects you can just dip into now and then through the years. And you only need to figure these into courses if you have external need to make up transcripts or report to government agencies.

And a final word: on occasion, textbooks can save planning time and they fit the comfort level of some families.

Well, that was a long answer. I hope you find help here in some of the thoughts.

*From God's World News, PO Box 2330, Asheville NC 28802, 800-951-5437.

**From The Voice of the Martyrs, PO Box 443, Bartlesville OK 74005, 918-337-8015.

Q. *My son is now entering high school and we want to know what to do to prepare for the PSAT and SAT tests. What do you think is the best method to prepare for them?*

A. My answer to the first question in this chapter lays out in generalities what a college bound student should accomplish during the high school years. Here are a few more specific pointers. You can use short versions of the tests for an indication of where your son's strong and weak areas are, and also for valuable experience with test taking. Teach your son to practice reading the questions before reading a selection; then he knows what to look for as he reads. This skill greatly increases a student's speed of working through the test.

These practice tests are available from several homeschool suppliers, also from college bookstores. Sign up to take the test in your junior year so you have one more year to work toward higher scores in the senior year test.

A good pre-test vocabulary builder is a study on Greek and Latin roots and prefixes and suffixes. You could begin this study any time during the teen years, but if you haven't, it still helps as a last minute cramming exercise according to students I have talked with.

Q. I read that you separate mechanics from grammar. Could you explain what you mean by mechanics, and how do we teach that at high school level?

A. By mechanics I mean punctuating, capitalizing and indenting. These enter into written language but not into speech. Grammar is the study of parts of speech, parts of sentences, and all the interrelations among these elements. There is yet a third category called usage. Usage includes matters like whether to write *home-schooler* as one word or two. In the 1980's there was much confusion over this, but with time and public usage the new word entered new dictionaries and it is no longer questioned. Usage also includes matters like when it's appropriate to use slang or informal wording, and when more formal wording is needed.

The main advantage in separating these in our thinking is that we can understand a policy of teaching mechanics as soon as children begin writing sentences, but not burdening them with grammar at that time. If it's all lumped together in people's minds, then they are puzzled, or horrified, when I advocate delaying grammar. It sounds as though I'm suggesting they delay teaching their children how to write.

Now for high schoolers, in general they should have mastered basic mechanics. More rare items will come up from time to time—items like indenting a quote, italicizing, parentheses, brackets, and so on. You can teach these in context. That is, teach something when the need for it arises.

For this purpose, I suggest using any standard college English handbook. This handbook should be in a convenient place near your largest dictionary. And, ideally, it should have been there since at least the junior high years of your oldest child. Before that, use a children's version of a handbook. By using such a handbook for reference over the years, your student will become familiar with its contents and how to find information in it. You can also use it as a textbook by studying a section in it now and then. Your student can carry this system into adult life, or into college if he goes. You'll eliminate the need for a series of graded English textbooks or workbooks with all their repetition. Even if you saved those books, you'd have a difficult time locating information that you want. And who likes looking through old, used workbooks, anyway?

If a student for some reason arrives at high school with poor writing mechanics, you can try the dictation method I describe at length in my books. Briefly, it consists of writing and studying one passage over several days until the student can write it from dictation without any errors. This requires close attention to details and should solve most problems for a teenager over a short period of time, maybe a few weeks.

Q. What are the essential writing skills that high school students need to learn? What kinds of writing should they be able to do?

A. I'd like to tell a story here about my older son at eighth grade. Complaining about footnoting, he said, "They tell us we'll need it in high school, then in high school they'll probably tell us we need it in college, just like they've been telling us in every grade that we need something for the next grade. Why can't they just let us be what we are now?"

I had to laugh. He was right, especially about footnoting. Students are required to footnote many reports along the way because they'll need to do that when they're in graduate school writing theses and dissertations. But in graduate school the footnoting details usually are made correct by hired typists, the people who love such details. So, is it essential to require footnoting mastery from everybody?

Our whole education establishment has spent millions recently to try to compile a list of essential outcomes in English and other areas. And you probably know how controversial they become as soon as any list is made public. So I decline to make my own list.

But I will comment. I should know something about writing.

I think that using models is the most direct way to improve writing. I call it the Benjamin Franklin method or the Jack London method, and it is my one-lesson writing course. My younger son used this method in high school to learn sports writing. He had the job of taking stats and other information from his games to the Anchorage newspaper so a staff member could write the stories. But Andy wanted to write the stories, so he typed the first one in the back of the car while we drove to town in the middle of night after the game. The next day he studied what changes had been made in his story. By the second game only a couple of changes were made. And by the third, he had become the writer for the games. They used his stories the rest of the season.

I could tell a similar experience about the first article I submitted to a magazine. I made my article sound like ones I saw in the magazine, and they published it with only one minor change.

Franklin used this method for non-fiction writing and London used it for fiction, so you can try it with any kind of writing you want your high schooler to do. I know that many homeschoolers enjoy various writing curriculums, and those help too. They can be another route to improved writing. These often analyze and break up writing into smaller tasks.

For instance, some lessons teach students to make more complex sentences by beginning with a clause, or other specific technique. And students do at times carry these ideas into their own writing the next day or the next week. On the other hand, students who read Dickens go to college writing such complex sentences that their professors know they have read Dickens. The modeling system at work again.

After making these comments about technique, I must add a word on the importance of having something to say. We can't expect our students to write a good story or good essay or good anything without first developing enough ideas and knowledge out of which to write.

Q. What do you think about speed reading at high school level?

A. I say yes, try it. Then I hasten to add that I don't necessarily recommend high priced courses that are advertised with hype and promises. Speed reading is not equal to speed learning as ads say. And thousands of words per minute is not the route to the top of the academic world. But on a commonsense level, improved reading skill is a major factor in good study skills.

Many people read at the speed of speech, which ranges around 300 words per minute. I would guess that this is true in homeschooling families which practice a lot of oral reading. A good first goal is to break the word-by-word habit and read at something over 400 words per minute.

Does the student move his lips? Or tongue? Or vocal cords in the neck? More difficult to determine is whether he mentally forms each word. The student himself must diagnose this. Once he is aware of that vocalization problem, he must concentrate on pushing himself past that word-by-word speed. With brief practice periods of high concentration he can determine to go faster than is comfortable and to keep going even if he misses some words. Use easy reading material for this practice.

He must also learn that his eye does not need to stop on each word. The eye can take in whole phrases at a time. It never needs to go to the end of a line because peripheral vision catches the outer edges. To practice this, you can use material like the "Reader's Digest," which has narrow columns. He can practice moving his eye down the columns, stopping just once per line. It may help to move a finger down the column and follow it with the eye. Practice forging ahead no matter what; break the habit of repeating a line or a sentence. These speed techniques require heightened concentration, and that leads to better comprehension than with slower speeds.

Books on speed reading have practice material for these and other techniques. The words in each selection are pre-counted for you and questions are provided so you can check on the comprehension. But good results can be obtained with your own practice material, too. To take timed reading tests in each practice session and keep records of improvement is highly motivating for students. In a few weeks most students will have broken over 400 words per minute and many students will have doubled their original speed.

Some highly touted courses that advertise thousands of words per minute use an opposite approach. Instead of gradually pushing the speed while continuing to comprehend the material, they teach rapid, rhythmical techniques of moving the eyes over the material, and gradually learning to comprehend it as they go. This is different from skimming. Skimming is a useful technique of looking through materials searching for a particular item or items. But with fast reading you're supposed to get everything as you go.

I have taught all these techniques in college courses, and some students in every class do, in fact, reach the phenomenal speeds you hear about. But almost no one likes it. They would not read novels that way. They cannot read textbook material that way. But they end up with a variety of techniques and speeds which they can use for a variety of purposes. And that is an ideal result for students. There is no one best way to read for all purposes.

10.
Issues of Family Life

God's First Institution— the Family

As homeschoolers, it doesn't take long for most people to figure out that some of the most perplexing issues you face are not related to academics. While you can find a text or guide for teaching your child to read, it may be hard to find help with issues such as family dynamics, outside comparisons of your children, and deciding the pace of teaching that is right for your family.

I have talked to many parents as I have traveled and spoken to homeschoolers. I know that these problems can seem difficult, sometimes overwhelming. You can also feel like you are the only person in the homeschooling world having these feelings. While the struggles are real, so is the help. We serve a faithful God, who hears our cries. When we can look past the struggle to the Lord, a way will often open of deliverance. Ruth gives us direction in how to look for those avenues of help and relief.

While Ruth readily states that her forte is curriculum, she gives us much insight in her answers to these questions. As a mother herself, she understands much of what we face as homeschoolers, and she gives us direction that is in keeping with her commonsense approach to solving problems.

—Debbie

Q. *What would be the best and most livable way to conduct a homeschool schedule with varied ages such as kindergarten, third grade and eighth grade. How many hours per day is reasonable per grade level?*

A. Each family has a different version of this question because of the varying ages of their children, and it is a major problem to work out as you begin homeschooling. To help make it livable, many families start with chores in the mornings, before and after breakfast. The house is put in order before the bookwork begins. Then a common schedule is to have about three hours of schoolwork during the morning, less for primary children. That's enough, ordinarily, to accomplish as much work as students in school do. But afternoons often are filled, too, with music practice, reading, community service or family ministry, library trips, family errands or work such as gardening, and so on. The eighth grader may work on a science project or other schoolwork that needs extra time.

In your case, remember that formal kindergarten is not necessary, as explained elsewhere in this book. So you will probably spend most of your teaching time with the third grader. The eighth grader will be able to study independently much of the time. So, theoretically it should all fit in. Naturally it helps if everybody is disciplined and kind, so make that a homeschooling goal to work toward.

Even with this age spread you could share some books together. Read aloud some Bible stories, Christian hero stories, historical fiction, and others. Work on Bible memory together. Besides family reading, the eighth grader can help the younger ones with arithmetic or anything. Teach all the children to help with meal preparation and cleanup or with laundry and other work that would make your day overfull if you tried to do it all yourself.

Q. Do you have any suggestions as to how to balance housework with doing school?

A. My area of writing is the schoolwork and not the housework, but I hear from homeschoolers how they manage. Mainly, you need to have an attitude of fitting everything into family life, rather than trying to add school on top of an already full load of housework. To accomplish this balance, the children must help with the work and the work can be considered part of school.

Preschool children can set the table, or sort laundry, fold clean laundry, match socks, and take clean laundry to the proper rooms. If they were at preschool they likely would use Montessori equipment to learn sorting and matching. These are thinking and observing skills. They also would learn at school how to put things away in their proper places.

Older children can help with cleaning, cooking, yard work, and numerous other tasks. Of course it takes a lot of teaching on your part to get them to the point where they are a real help to you, but that's the school part. It's better to learn family and home skills in the real setting than to learn them in home economics and other classes.

Read some of the books written by home-school moms and you will find many wonderful, creative ideas for fitting all this together.

Q. How do you handle it when a younger sibling exceeds in a specific subject and it causes the older one to think he is dumb?

A. If there can be any solution to this kind of problem, I think the key is in the attitude of the teacher and other adults around the children. Try looking for occasions to speak of good actions and good traits about both your children. These can be little things—removing muddy shoes, doing a job unasked, answering the phone politely. Concerning school work, comment on items that do not measure or compare ability, like keeping their materials in order, starting without complaining or wasting time, sticking with a job to completion, and so on. Then when it's time for the hard subject, treat it matter-of-factly. It's no big deal that Buddy has an easier assignment; that's what he needs right now.

If the troublesome subject is reading, it often is because Buddy has an eye or other neurological problem that makes reading more difficult for him now. It is good to help the children understand the problem and realize that Buddy will read better later on.

The older sibling should catch his attitude from you. If he doesn't, if he makes disparaging comments about Buddy, then set him straight. "Buddy is working hard; are you working hard too?" He should realize that you don't want to hear those disparaging comments. Help the children act as friends and talk about how they will still be friends when they are grown up.

This is life. People all around us have varying abilities in everything. Your children are now in training, learning how to deal with this.

Q. How can we move into a homeschooling lifestyle of learning, more relaxed and enjoyable?

A. I think it works best to move gradually from what you are presently doing toward the model that you have seen or envision. One reason is that the children need to learn how to use new freedom. For instance, when you have trained your children to choose library books and care for books and put them in their place after use, then you could have free reading time in your schedule. When your children know which tools they are allowed to use and know the safety rules and cleanup rules, then they could have free time with Dad's tools, or with Mom's kitchen equipment, or your science equipment, or whatever. Free time outdoors is wonderful if you don't have to worry about the social services people.

Those free times are slightly structured, simply by calling them "free time" and by allotting a specified length of time. Eventually your children may be pursuing projects in their free time that seem to you quite worthwhile. Then you can be the cheerleader. Get more materials, more information, a new idea, whatever will help them to go farther than they would on their own. Along the way you can quit using some of the textbooks; they're likely to seem superfluous if things are going well.

This gradual approach has the advantage that you, as well as the children, can feel comfortable. You won't drop all the books at once and then months later say, "Oh, we should have continued with the arithmetic book."

But there are other routes. If you and the children want a sudden change, you could sit and plan. Lay out some long range goals, starting with a week or a month. Later, the children may learn to think in terms of a year or more, as, "I want to learn to play violin this year." You can insist on certain parameters, such as that they must read so many books per month. Plan a family ministry together, such as organizing the church library or ministering to sick or elderly people. Plan how your own family work will be accomplished.

The gradual route to change or the sudden route—both can work, so take your choice.

Q. How would you deal with a very bright child who continues to "hate" school. We read to him constantly and go ahead with school.

A. The way you are now dealing with it is a perfectly good choice until you figure out a next step. I would want to know whether hate is a word and attitude he picked up from peers. If so, that's a separate—non-academic—problem to work on.

If you assess that it's really a problem with the academic work, you could experiment with new ideas one at a time. Choose an idea that you like that you've heard from another family or that you read, and try it. Look especially for some active work on a project as a contrast to doing worksheets. (I am assuming this child is primary age, because you read to him regularly.)

If he is older than primary you could try asking, "If we don't do this history book, what would you do for history instead?" He will probably need time to think about it and need some ideas from you. But if he ends up helping plan his history learning, you're on your way to developing a more motivated learner.

Q. My 6-year-old son Michael has an inability to focus or stay on track with school work or chores. He has no problem focusing on a book or other project he's interested in. At what point, and how, do I teach him responsibility for himself so that he can be left alone to do a job without supervision? Am I expecting too much for now? It's hard to walk the line between his age and his mental abilities. I have not had him tested, but believe he is gifted.

A. I think that most parents would feel that six years of age is quite young to expect very much independent work and responsibility, even if the child is academically advanced. He should learn to complete short jobs within his ability. You can praise him when he does, and as he grows older the size of such independent work will grow with him. One teaching idea is to work alongside Michael on some jobs. Be the model of working cheerfully and carefully, and of being happy when the job is well done.

Q. My 8-year-old daughter has a tough time in Christian prep school. She seems to be lost in a school that teaches to the top student, because she is very creative and dramatic. After prayer my jusband and I decided that homeschooling would be better for her. We plan to start in the fall semester, but I am a little scared. Should I try to start in the summer, so I can take time off in October to have a new baby? Or am I biting off more than I can chew? I currently work to help put her through private school.

A. If you are only a little scared, you already are miles ahead of most beginning homeschoolers. And trading the workplace for time at home with your daughter and new baby should be a good trade. So scared or not, I say go ahead with your plan.

It wouldn't hurt to begin in the summer. With an early start, you may be able to relax more and just have a parttime summer school atmosphere. Try to make your daughter's homeschool experience different from her school experience. Be less structured. Give her opportunity to express her creativity. And for yourself, don't expect to get everything figured out before you begin. You can add and change things all you want as you go along.

Q. *I have a 16-year-old son who is a junior in high school. He's having trouble with school. Is it appropriate to begin homeschooling him at this time?*

A. Yes, it's appropriate to begin at any time your family wishes. Especially if your son himself wants to homeschool, you are far ahead of where some families are when they realize they should remove children from their school situation.

Q. *If boys do not play football in school, how will they learn to enjoy watching football games?*

A. That's an interesting question, and its ramifications go far beyond football. In every stadium crowd are fans at all degrees of understanding and enjoyment. Probably a minority have played on teams where fans watched them. Others played flag football or sandlot versions of various levels of sophistication. And others, especially women, did not play at all. Yet there they are, cheering together.

Those with the best experience in the skills and the most knowledge of strategy no doubt experience deeper enjoyment than those around them. But put the same crowd at a concert the next week and the scores are overturned. Now the ones who performed music and understand it are on top.

So what's a parent to do? Get his child onto every team and into every activity? No, that's not necessary, because certain learnings carry over from one field to others. When a student puts long effort into a skill and works with a team or ensemble and then achieves a good game or performance, he can better appreciate the achievement of others.

So each student should pursue to a high level the skills in which he is interested or has aptitude. And, in addition, he should be exposed at the sandlot level to a wide variety of other skills. It's at the sandlot where you and he discover whether to pursue something further. And it's at the sandlot where he learns enough about different activities to be able to appreciate others who achieve in them.

In one sense we could say that most of elementary and secondary education is the sandlot—the opportunity to try everything and to choose some areas to rise higher than sandlot ability.

Q. Do you have any tips for teaching an only child?

A. On this kind of question you might get more help from other parents in this situation than from me. Try trading ideas in a support group. It seems to me that your biggest problem would be the lack of the synergy that develops where several people study together. So you might search for ways to provide some of this. Occasional co-op activities could help, especially the kind which require work in between the meetings. That is, if the children write poems or prepare science demonstrations or something at home and then present them at meetings, they get the extra motivation of an anticipated audience and the learning from others that helps motivate their next efforts, and so on, hopefully building up more synergy with time.

Q. We tend to have a light structure with much freedom of choice within our homeschool. But I have been reading about and trying to relax my methods. Yet I saw character flaws being fed (laziness, lack of vision, idleness). Or is this just childishness? My oldest (13) flourishes in this and most environments. The almost 12-year-old approaches most things with a "just tell me the minimum requirement." Do you see any relationship between structure and character?

A. This sounds to me like a situation where mother knows best. You can read your daughter's heart better than anyone. If your younger daughter needs more structure and your older daughter doesn't, treat them differently. As the younger one grows, and you give her the structure she needs, she may develop more ambition and self-motivation.

Concerning your question about the relationship with character, I haven't seen any research on this. There is an old classic research on learning and structure. The result was that just as much learning happened either way. So, according to that, you could get good learning results with both girls, treating them differently.

Q. My son is entering fifth grade. He loves to read but doesn't really have a love for learning. We've been homeschooling since kindergarten. Any ideas for nurturing a true love for learning?

A. I'm baffled by this question, because reading and learning are so intertwined. By reading, your son is learning. I wonder if by learning you are referring to something specific, like doing school assignments, or completing a science experiment to answer a question. In general, children are born to learn. It is often stated that they explore and learn constantly until we confine them in our classrooms and gradually turn off their learning traits and motivations. Also in general, it helps if children are in families where learning attitudes are a way of life, on outings, while working, and all other non-book activities, as well as in sharing books.

But generalities may not solve your individual problem. Many families have solved a problem like this by searching for a topic or activity the child is interested in, and using it as an entry point for further learning. It could be something like horseback riding or raising a pet. These require learning how to care for the animal and feed it. It could expand to learning about nutrition and medical aspects, about breeds and breeding, history of the animal, riding skills, competition, ranching and herding, and on and on.

Every interest you try won't become a full-blown, comprehensive project. Some may interest for a day, and others longer. But a major goal through the school years should be to expose children to a wide range of topics and activities. Some few children will find early the interest they will pursue throughout a lifetime. Most will find one or more interests later on.

Many of these lifetime interests grow not out of the children's choices but simply out of a school topic they were required to study. So, take heart, you are early in the process with a fifth grader.

Q. What is a proper response to family members when they compare other children the same age to yours who may not be reading, etc.?

A. I think there is no response invented yet that will convince an unbeliever (in home-schooling) quickly. With a delayed reader, your main responsibility is to protect him from the pressure and disapproval of unbelievers. Quietly go about your own family work, don't argue too much, and patiently wait for the time when your success will argue for itself.

Q. My son is a second grader and not really reading yet. I want to know how I can cope with his Sunday school which is very schoolish and academically oriented. They do round-robin reading, fill out worksheets, etc. The teacher is critical of my child and of my approach to teaching him. The pressure this situation creates for us as a family is very great. We don't want to withdraw from the fellowship of the Sunday school class, yet we don't want our child to feel inferior or like a failure.

A. I see this as a serious problem that should not exist at all. The teachers and the curriculum should make allowances for individual differences in children and especially for a 7-year-old boy who's not reading. There are lots of those.

I suppose the first thing to try is discussing the problem with the teacher and working out some adjustment. But it sounds as if you've already done that, and she disagrees with your view.

The next choice is for you to figure out some other alternative. Maybe he can visit a sibling's class where he mostly listens. Maybe he can sit with you in an adult class. Maybe you can talk with the Christian education director about what could be done. Maybe your family can skip Sunday school for a year or so, just going for church. I know some families have even taken the drastic step of changing churches, but this is not a forever problem, so that is pretty drastic.

These suggestions assume that you just will not allow your son to go through the humiliation of being a non-reader in this situation. Some few children may have a personality that can handle that. But one of the reasons you homeschool is so your children can grow and learn at their own pace. You're protecting this 7-year-old from what would happen to him in many schools, and now it seems you must protect him from your Sunday school, too. Hopefully, churches will learn from the homeschoolers and this situation will become more rare in the future.

I must caution that these Sunday school problems should not degenerate into situations where the homeschooler is always right. I'd like to tell about a third grade girl who cried each week when it was time for Sunday school. Her mother said, "You don't have to like it, but I expect you to handle it. Without crying." She further explained that God gave that teacher the job of teaching the class, and she worked hard to prepare the lesson. Then together they prayed for the teacher and the girl and the class just before piling into the car with the rest of the family. A dramatic turnaround followed. As I recall, the girl "handled" Sunday school one week and by the second week was fully enjoying it.

Q. I would appreciate input on handling the socialization issue for my son. He attended public school until middle of fourth grade. He is now in seventh grade and is very happy being homeschooled. He met his best friend the first day of kindergarten and they've been close ever since—until now. His best friend doesn't call anymore. My son asked what's wrong, but he never gets a straight answer.

I am trying to find some activities where my son is around other children, but it isn't always easy. He doesn't like sports, so that isn't an option. We've just started attending a new church, so hopefully he can meet some nice boys. He's starting an art class next week and is signed up for a homeschool Spanish class.

I have prayed hard for the Lord to guide my son through this. He is a sweet, kind boy and that actually seems to cause him trouble with some kids. I don't want him to feel that being a nice person is a bad thing. It sure doesn't help that his best friend lives just over the fence.

A. Much as we would like to, we parents cannot shield our children from all the hurts of life. One comfort for us adults is to know that children's character is strengthened by coming successfully through a trial like this. Later the child, too, may see this. I would say that you're doing a good job of supporting your son, praying, and guiding him to get on with his own life in spite of his loss and disappointment.

And who knows how this will end? You both may eventually be glad that the friendship was broken off. Could it be that the friend is now getting into activities and friendships that he cannot share with a nice boy from a Christian family? Or it could have a more happy ending. But in any case, with the way you are handling it, your son will be a stronger and a better friend than ever to this boy or to whomever the Lord sends as friends for him.

Q. *Due to shared custody, we are unable to homeschool our 9-year-old third grade son. However, we'd like to homeschool him over our half of the summer, focusing primarily on reading skills, to better prepare him for fourth grade. Can you suggest any particular curriculum or program that would work well in a situation such as this?*

A. This seems to me a perfect situation for using an informal approach. More learning will happen with a little cuddly bedtime reading than with twice as much "school" reading during the day. What third graders need most is lots of reading from easy books. So have books around the house. Take trips to the library, combined with a pizza or ice cream outing. Read to your son. Read with him; that is, you read your book and he reads his, side-by-side. And when he gets ready to leave, visit a bookstore where he chooses a book or two to own and take with him. Don't overdo the reading, but try some ideas that you think will work smoothly in the few weeks that you have.

Be sure you manage time for climbing trees and rocks, riding a bike, wading in a cold stream, and other such timeless boyhood activities. These are important for both physical and mental development.

As for other schoolwork besides reading, you could keep that informal too. Have your son help your husband work on the car, or build or repair anything. Learn something about map reading and understanding traffic patterns while you're going places in the car. Take simple field trips, but don't call them that. Visit local businesses where products are made or grown, and treat these trips like vacation outings. Spending time together, talking and doing things, makes for a language rich environment. Maybe the boy can make a friend that he wants to write to after he returns to his other home.

Call this a classroom without walls if you want to. That's a popular education term. A few happy weeks in this real-life classroom should send him into fourth grade better prepared than a summer of workbooks or other structured curriculum.

Q. I am a single parent and believe I am supposed to be homeschooling my child. My child has been through a lot this year, and I think the time together, as well as the lower stress level will help us both. I can make the time, schedule-wise, with help from my family, but I wanted to know what you thought of this. I don't know any other single parents who homeschool, yet I can't deny my feeling led to do this. My family is fairly supportive, though they consider this an unusual step. Do you have any guidance for me?

A. I would just say yes, go ahead. With your desire and with family support you can manage. Others have. I have met a few single moms at homeschool meetings. They all were smiling, happy people. Some were leaders in the groups. And if someone hadn't told me privately about the difficult financial or other struggles of these moms, I would not have known their situation was any different from the others.

You didn't say whether your child is a boy or girl, but especially if it's a boy you should be looking for male role models for him. Maybe an uncle or someone in the family will work in the garage with him, take him fishing and so forth. Other possibilities are the child's Sunday school teacher or other church member, scoutmaster, or athletic coach. And definitely get into a homeschool support group. These are all busy people, but they do support one another.

I'd like to suggest to any homeschool father reading this, that if you have single moms in your group you should consider the ministry you could have to the sons, and daughters too, in these families. Just inviting them occasionally to join your family in an outing will help more than you know.

Debbie's Note: I must take this opportunity to encourage those among you who are single parent homeschoolers (men and women), or grandparent homeschoolers, or aunt homeschoolers. I am meeting more and more of you who have accepted the responsibility for these children, and who are now taking on their educational needs as well. Your dedication and sacrifice has been inspiring to me! When you share with me your desire to do what you feel God is calling you to do, in spite of the obstacles you face, I am blessed and encouraged, and so should you be. God's love for your children is no less than His love for anyone else's, so you can be confident that He will lead you to do what is best for them. Thank you for your devotion to your children and your obedience to the Lord. It is an inspiration to us all.

Q. *Can you tell us a little about your testimony and how you were led into what you are doing today?*

A. After a long life it is difficult to tell a little, but I'll try. I was saved as a child so young that I have no memory of being without God. I always knew He was "up there" and I could talk to Him. I assume that this was due either to a preschool Sunday school teacher or to my grandmother, both of whom were the kind of Christians who would lead a child to Christ. My own family were more quiet Christians. We children walked to a nearby country church, where we learned Bible stories, memorized verses, sang in choir and made lifelong friends.

ISSUES OF
FAMILY LIFE

When I was a teenager, one day I read Philippians 4:8 about thinking on the good, beautiful and true. I immediately connected that with the famous line that a leading nutritionist of the day closed his radio program with regularly: Remember, you are what you eat. I reasoned that whatever I put into my mind would be the material that God would have to work with to make the future me. I hadn't heard then of taking a life verse, but looking back now I can say that that has always been my life verse.

Through the influence of Christian high school teachers, I ended up going to a small Christian college along with several high school friends. That was a rich experience, everything we would like to see from Christian colleges today. I grew much in my Christian life.

One day the college president led a meeting on finding God's will for our lives. I remember him telling that he didn't decide as a young person that he would be a college president when he grew up. In fact, his father was disappointed when he went first into construction work instead of teaching. He did later teach, and I think, preach, and then became president of the college, where his construction background helped with college building programs. My experience is somewhat similar.

I started out teaching and, because of moving around, gained experience in large and small schools, rich and poor, minority and white, and all grades. Then I began teaching college education courses, including supervising student teachers. I thought, this is why the Lord gave me such broad teaching experiences. He knew I needed that background for teaching teachers. Then I worked as writer and editor in a company producing curriculum for churches. There I thought, this is why the Lord gave me experience teaching children of all ages, and teachers as well. He knew I needed that background for writing curriculum. Now I write and publish for homeschoolers and I think, this is why...

In that brief story I didn't take space to tell about mistakes and failures and trials, and about hard work. All of those, too, provide background out of which I try to help homeschoolers.

How did I get into homeschooling? I was in the publishing industry when I first saw this movement coming along. To me it seemed natural, what I would have done with my own two sons if I had been born a bit later. This was the best and healthiest movement in education. I tried, with my own company and with others, to interest someone in producing the kind of materials I thought would fit family education, and I could find no one willing to break so far from the traditional mold. So without the backing of a publisher, I wrote *The Three R's* and *You CAN Teach Your Child Successfully.* And I watch with great pleasure as homeschooling families themselves produce more and more of the mold-breaking materials.

May God continue to bless and guide you all in the great work you are doing for Him.

Q. What do you see as the greatest benefit to

homeschooling? At times in the midst of seeing good kids in school, it's hard to remember why we go through this.

A. Probably the greatest benefit is the character you can build into your children by spending so much time with them. You can instill your own values and worldview and spiritual outlook and so forth, without the intrusion of contrary teaching and unwholesome peer influence.

I can't deny that some children manage to thrive spiritually in a school setting, and perhaps yours would, too. But benefits of homeschooling accrue to you, as well as to your children. You are bonding with them now as children, and they will become your best friends as adults. Also you have a chance to relearn the stuff you have forgotten from your own school days. When your children's school years have passed, they will seem as a brief span of years. Live them well and fully.

11.
Testing and Special Education

Making Servants Out of Masters

One of the things I have done for many years is administer achievement tests to children. I did this as a special education teacher, and was part of many special education staffing meetings. Later, as a homeschooler, I began doing achievement testing and evaluations here in Florida fulfilling that requirement of our homeschooling law. Though the situations are different, many common denominators are the same. One is parents who want or need information about their children's academic performance and are asking someone in the education profession for their assistance.

Often the problem with all this for homeschoolers is keeping it in perspective. Without other sources of information, especially ones you trust, the information you are given can seem overwhelming, or even intimidating. With situations like a learning problem or testing, it seems like the normal thing to do to give much of the decision-making power over to others, but it should not be so. Testing and the services offered by professionals are tools to use, servants of your homeschooling efforts. Keeping that perspective is crucial to wisely using the information they give you.

In this chapter, Ruth offers advice on handling testing and learning questions with just the right perspective. These situations can be trying, and the approach she takes to addressing these concerns is one of calmness and confidence. As a longtime educational problem solver, Ruth knows that there is help for your situation, and she gives you great direction in finding that help.

—Debbie

Q. At what point should a parent become concerned about reading and what clues do I look for to determine if there is a reading problem?

A. I am reluctant to give specific ages, because each child is different, and there is such a wide range, with children beginning to read at 3 or at 12. But I will say that 7 1/2 is the average age at which boys have the mental and verbal development to catch on easily to reading instruction. Girls, up to about one year earlier.

So if your child is not beginning to read at the average starting time, yet seems to have normal mental ability, you naturally wonder what to do. Should you wait and see if he is a late bloomer who will suddenly read at 12, or should you be searching for a possible problem?

I think it's best to start searching for a problem you can solve. Though your child may outgrow his problem and suddenly read at 12, you don't know that ahead of time. He may not.

About ten percent of children have neurological problems severe enough to interfere with reading. Sometimes you can detect this by their frowning and squinting, or very short attention to close work, or by continued reversals of letters or words. You also can check for left-right dominance. If the child is right-handed, does he have a matching right dominance in eye, ear and foot? If there is any mixture of dominance it can cause a sort of scrambling of messages in the brain. Dominance problems are often solved by physical exercises designed for the purpose. Some books or convention speakers give information about this.

Eye problems are of several types, and only a small percentage of eye doctors help on these. I can't count the times a parent of a struggling reader has said to me, "We've had her eyes checked, and they're fine." The typical vision check-up does not uncover problems of focusing, or of letters that swim around or reverse, or other common reading problems. It's important to locate an eye doctor listed as a vision therapist. Then it's also important to determine whether the doctor will give you exercises and treatments to carry out at home, or whether he insists on the more expensive route of doing everything in his office.

Beyond the neurological problems, another ten percent of children have learning problems caused by dietary or environmental factors. Many doctors in alternative medicine today can test and help track down these.

There is no simple set of clues to list. But if your child is beyond average reading age and not catching on to reading instruction, then almost anything that persists, that strikes you as not quite normal, could be a clue to inquire about. Fortunately, today in most areas your network of homeschool contacts can lead you to further help, or on the other hand, can assure you when it's not time to worry yet.

Debbie's Note: I have often referred homeschooling parents to a book entitled Helping Children Overcome Learning Difficulties *by Jerome Rosner. It is published by Walker and Company, and is subtitled "A Step by Step Guide for Parents and Teachers." It is a wonderfully practical book that can help you evaluate your children yourself, and then help you form your own plan of attack. It is available from the public library. If your library doesn't have it, see if they can obtain it for you through an inter-library loan program.*

Q. When my son, Jon, came along, I assumed teaching reading was a breeze because my daughter, Heather, had caught on quickly and seemed to develop her own system. I started teaching him at 5 1/2 as I had Heather. I quickly determined he was not ready and waited one year, and another. Now he has just turned nine and his reading is labored. He just throws out guesses when he sees the first letter or tries to sound out sight words that he has read for years and should know by now.

His last two achievement tests weren't good. He scored about the 20th percentile in reading. He is a whiz in math. I know he is smart and verbally gifted.

Is it time to be alarmed? I guess I just want to know when I should get help with reading. How long should I wait? How do I know if he will grow or mature into reading or if I need to seek reading help?

A. Since Jon is now 9 and since you say he's smart in other things, it sounds as if you should be searching for a solution rather than just waiting. Homeschoolers have inspiring stories of keeping children productive and happy until they begin reading at a late age. But, as I mentioned in the preceding answer, you don't know ahead of time whether you'll have that happy ending by just waiting.

One thing you can check is the achievement test scores. There may be a subsection of reading which is called "vocabulary," where the tester reads the items aloud. If there is no vocabulary score, find out which section on that test was oral. That score can be considered roughly equivalent to "reading capacity." Is this higher than Jon's other reading subscores? In other words, this may confirm your assessment that Jon's mental understanding is higher than his reading ability.

So the question is: what keeps Jon from reading up to the level of his verbal capacity? The guessing and inability to recognize sight words could be hints of some kind of eye problem. These are explained a little in the reading chapter, and it would be good to locate a vision therapist who can diagnose and help you treat these problems. Another possibility is mixed dominance, which can often be corrected with exercises. Since the eyes are probably involved in any dominance problem the vision therapist may also help to give you treatment options on this. A new term some people use for the dominance treatments is "brain integration."

By networking among your homeschool organizations and checking on conference speakers, you can often locate more information and help on these usually correctable problems. I would caution that, as with everything else, there are people who charge far too much and see homeschoolers as a lucrative market. Your defense is to learn as much as you can from reading and from the specialists you talk with. Those who are free with information and who give you treatments to carry out at home, along with what they may have to do in their offices, are the ones to work with.

Q. My 8-year-old daughter has struggled with reading from the start. One day my husband gave her a spelling test and I forgot to tell him that she used primary lined paper and that I numbered the page for her. Instead, he gave her a sheet of college lined paper. Afterwards, he showed me her test, thinking that she had misspelled all the words. It took a few minutes to find that she had spelled all the words correctly. You simply had to hold the page up to a mirror to read it! Everything was written in a perfect mirror image, starting on the right side, numbers and all!

At that time we decided not to have her tested for learning disorders since she was making progress and we didn't want to see her labeled. Now I wonder if we made the right decision. I went to the library and researched her problem the best I could and made some changes such as letting her use a blank, white card as a marker under the line when she is reading. Do you think we should have some testing done, and if so, what type?

A. I wish we had space to print all of this interesting letter. I admire the patience and resourcefulness of parents like you. In my early years of teaching I knew less about reading problems than most homeschool moms of today. You certainly have done a great job so far and have analyzed quite well what your daughter can and cannot do.

It seems to me that there's no need to spend time and money on testing that will end up with someone saying, "Yes, your daughter has a problem with reversals," or other information that you know already. Now if someone thinks he can cure her reversal problem, that's another story. I believe that 90% can be cured or greatly improved by eye exercises or other treatment as indicated for each case. The 10% that cannot be cured are usually hereditary. Does a parent or uncle or other relative have this condition? If you decide it's probably not hereditary, then I suggest pursuing treatment as described in the preceding answer.

If you decide this is not treatable, then do what you can to prepare your daughter for a life that doesn't depend heavily on reading. People do this all the time. Many engineers, for instance, gravitated to that field precisely because they were dyslexic and could handle math courses better than the history or literature courses. Help your daughter understand that though reading is harder for her than for most people, she can with hard work eventually learn to read. Keep the teaching sessions short. Use kinesthetic methods and the other techniques you have already found helpful. And let her spend more time on things she does well than on those which may make her too discouraged with herself and her school work.

Q. I have a hard time getting my 7-year-old daughter to do any school work because she has a very strong imagination. Everything comes alive—pencils, pictures, particles floating in the air. Any suggestions?

A. This question reminds me of some research of a Russian neuropsychologist named A.R. Luria. He had a subject with a remarkable memory because his mind made images of everything. We often hear about the higher percentage of information we remember from seeing versus hearing. I don't believe the percentages, but that's another topic. What I want to point out here is that if we notice and retain images of everything, it interferes with our thinking.

Here's Luria's subject explaining his problems with reading the sentence, "The work got underway normally." *As for* work, *I see that work is going on...there's a factory....But there's that word* normally. *What I see is a big, ruddy-cheeked woman, a normal woman...then the expression* get underway. *Who? What is all this? You have industry...that is a factory, and this normal woman...but how does all this fit together? How much I have to get rid of just to get the simple idea of the thing!*

The images collided with one another and produced chaos. If the sentence was read aloud to the subject, then the voice intruded as another blur and muddled the meaning still more.

For a child with more vivid imaging than average, work at cutting out as much visual intrusion as possible. Construct a study carrel which blocks the view straight ahead and on both sides. A simple one can be made quickly by cutting a cardboard carton to form the three walls, and stand it on a desktop. Then hunt for books with no color or pictures. In today's world you probably won't find enough of these, and you'll have to resort to cutting out parts to use. Try having the child sit at the carrel with just one sheet to read, or maybe with one worksheet and a pencil. Experiment until you find an arrangement that she can handle.

If you work along this line and find that this over-imaging is indeed your daughter's problem, then teach a lot from real life rather than from books. Luria's subject knew what a factory is, and I would assume he didn't learn that from reading about factories. The man was a reporter whose boss noticed his phenomenal memory. Until the boss suggested he be evaluated by a psychologist, he didn't realize he was different from most everybody else. Who knows what God has in store for your uniquely talented daughter?

Q. *I have an 8-year-old boy who is weak in language arts, particularly spelling. He was tested by the public school and was found to need extra help. Should I let the school help or just get ideas from them and help him on my own?*

A. I think all homeschoolers reading this will join me in urging you to help your son on your own. The best language development comes from interaction with adults. You can converse with your child and read to him for more time each day than any classroom teacher can. Oral language and good pronunciation come first, then reading and writing.

I wouldn't worry much about spelling until after your child reads fluently—about fourth grade level. You can work hard at spelling then, and he will learn it more easily at that time. In the meantime just work once in a while on words he uses frequently and at important occasions such as a letter to grandmother.

Q. *How important is it to give my 9- and 12-year-old children tests over the material we are studying?*

A. This kind of test is useful only when you have a particular use for it. You won't need to test routinely as in classrooms, because in most cases you already know how much of the material the children have learned, and because you don't need to collect artificial scores like this in order to compute artificial grades. Sometimes you can use tests for motivation or for accountability, as when you tell the children to study a chapter and get ready to pass a test on it. Other times you may use tests to show mastery of speed or accuracy, as with a timed test of multiplication facts. Still other times, you may use a test as a way to review or to determine whether you need to review something.

You may find other uses besides these, but in general you will probably use tests rarely as compared with schools because your tutoring situation is so different from the classroom situation.

Q. What do standardized test scores really say about what the children know or don't know? What should you do with the results?

A. There are two major kinds of tests. One is called "norm referenced." That means the scores refer you to norms, and norms come from scoring masses of students (the same root as normal). The concept of norms is as simple as the concept of average. Average is a norm, figured from averaging out the scores of a population of students. Other scores, such as grade levels or percentile ranks, spread above and below the average.

When I was a classroom teacher these scores told me little new. I already knew which students would score high and which would score low or in between. And the parents usually already knew about their children also. Homeschooling parents more often feel a need for these scores, because they don't know how their children would rank among a group of children, and they don't even have a report card sent by a teacher who does have a group of children.

But then there's the philosophical problem of whether we should be comparing our children with other children. If your child is struggling with reading, do you really need a comparative score, or is it enough to know that you and he are doing the best you can at the present time? Or if the child is an excellent reader and loves to read, does someone need a high score as a feather in his cap? You may need it to fend off your critics of homeschooling. About all you can do with test results is to notice in which areas your child is lower than you would like, so you can plan to emphasize those areas in the coming year.

Each child doesn't need to be high in everything. One long-time school principal received resounding applause from his whole town when he stated, "I don't care whether all our students are good in science as long as our scientists are good in science."

The other major kind of standardized test is the standards based test. (They used to be called criterion referenced tests.) These score according to whether or not the student shows the knowledge or the skill that was set up as a standard. For instance, a standard might be that the student knows from memory the times tables. This is the sort of test the whole nation has been fighting over, trying to reach agreement on what the standards should be. If a standard is that the child can write a good paragraph, the scoring is not as simple as with the times tables. It takes a committee of teachers to decide whether a paragraph rates as "proficient" or some lower level. And already in one district the teachers changed their criteria of what it took to rate a paragraph proficient. They said they could toughen it up next year when the schools have more time to get used to this system of evaluation.

So if your child is going to be evaluated with a standards based test, you would want to know what the standards are and whether you agree with them. Also, you really should know these in advance so you can teach to those particular standards. That's what the schools are supposed to do. But if you know a standard, and you agree with it and teach it, then you know when the child accomplishes it, and you have no need to subject him to a mass test.

The more you reason like this about standardized tests the less it seems that you need them. At the beginning, mass tests were to evaluate schools to see if they were doing their jobs. The tests were not meant to be used so individually, especially as the basis for high stakes decisions about individuals.

Q. What do you think about left-brain and right-brain learning?

A. I think a lot of hocus-pocus has spread concerning this. My basic statement is that God has not left us floundering these thousands of years using half our brains until modern science came along to tell us how to use the rest.

What happened was that neurologists were publishing new discoveries about brain anatomy and neurology, and educators jumped on this information with premature theories about how it affects learning. This hit the public fancy and some best-selling books resulted. Some people are always looking for ways to help the future evolution of mankind, and this was more promising than anything they had seen in a while.

After a decade or two, responsible educators could see that their theories were not working as hoped. Excitement waned. Articles debunking the theories appeared. But the popular literature, and the Christian education literature, unfortunately, are not pulled off the shelves as easily. So this idea lingers.

Now, having said all that, I will add that there is something to using the right-brain knowledge in solving certain learning problems. This is not recent information, but it has long been known that sensory input from the right side of the body goes to the left side of the brain, and vice versa. Thus if your child is writing a word with his dominant right hand while looking at it with his dominant left eye leading, the hand and eye messages are not coordinated properly in the brain. But that's a different story than the learning theories.

Q. *I'm really struggling with Erick, my 8-year-old. He has a slight speech problem (enunciation of two or more syllable words and other blends), and seems to forget short* i *and* e *sounds. He has been diagnosed as being ADHD. We try to keep from giving him the Ritalin as prescribed by doctors, due to possible future problems. I would really appreciate and welcome your comments.*

A. First, I will say that short *i* and *e* sounds are difficult for most children, and for that reason I suggest teaching short *e* last, after the other short vowel sounds are learned quite well. And a child with a speech problem is likely to have more than average difficulty with sounds. Erick is only 8, so I think you need not be overly worried yet. Continue using any and all approaches that you have for teaching reading. Work on sounds and difficult items for brief periods, and allow longer periods of easy reading.

As to ADHD, I think you're right to avoid Ritalin. In fact, if the problems you mention in your letter are the most serious you have, I see no reason to consider medicine of any kind. If Erick has attention problems and hyperactivity problems, then I think the first step is to check with a nutritionally oriented doctor. Some doctors are convinced that the epidemic of ADHD is related to our modern environment of pesticides, food additives and such. A good book on this is *Help for the Hyperactive Child* by Dr. William G. Crook.

Besides looking into foods, look into nutritional supplements. Dianne Craft (address at end of chapter) tells me that sometimes mineral supplements are calming. Sometimes homeopathic remedies. Study into these areas or find experienced help. I'm convinced that the solution for many children can be found this way.

Also, I will mention an alternative to Ritalin, which is phenytoin (PHT), known by the brand name Dilantin, manufactured by Parke-Davis. Although the medical encyclopedia lists practically the same side effects for this as for Ritalin, it has been used for most of a century without any problems. The reason we don't hear about it these days is that the patent has expired and Ritalin is what gets marketed to the doctors. Dilantin does not sedate as does Ritalin. Instead, it seems to normalize the electro-chemical functions of the nervous system.

Q. I have a child the school system labels ADD. I've chosen to help him learn skills, but often feel guilty that perhaps I make him struggle in areas that Ritalin would allow him to focus in more easily. Are there any findings on long term with Ritalin versus without?

A. I haven't seen any studies in those particular terms. But information is coming out about addiction and other problems with long term use. The armed forces will not accept applicants who have used Ritalin within the previous six years. Many children outgrow their ADD symptoms. Those who don't will learn along the way how to cope with their problem, and they will become our firemen and wilderness guides and such. So the best course seems to be to continue to struggle as you are without medication. If you do decide on medication, look into the alternative Dilantin mentioned in the preceding answer.

Q. My 11-year-old daughter is at second to third grade level in reading and math and at about a 5- to 6-year-old emotional level. She has a poor short term memory. 1) How do parents tell when they have a slow learner and when they have a child with a learning difficulty? Is there a test? 2) Where are these children when they reach their twenties? Has any research shown how well adjusted they are as adults, especially in comparison with how their problem was treated?

A. On question one, it sounds as if you have already diagnosed that your daughter's general development is slow and her mental development pretty much matches. Unless you have good reason to believe that she should be learning faster, I do not recommend running around to specialists and getting tests.

On the important second question, every year homeschoolers are bringing in more evidence that academic achievement is not the whole of life. Employers value responsibility, good work habits, loyalty, cheerfulness and other character traits they find in homeschoolers. I buy healthy bread at a bakery that is a wonderful, cheerful place to enter, and I have no idea what grades the lady behind the counter made in school. Give your daughter time to work at what she does well, and don't spend too much time with what frustrates her and makes her feel like a failure.

Debbie's Note: A good source for materials for such children is American Guidance Services. They produce curriculum that has regular grade level content (such as biology, world history, English, etc.) but is written on approximately a fourth grade reading level. For a student who doesn't read well, but also wants to work independently, this is a great find. Here is their address, from which you can request a catalog of basic skills materials: American Guidance Service, 4201 Woodland Road (PO Box 99), Circle Pines MN 55014-1796. Phone: 800-328-1560.

Q. What is the best source of basic skills to teach? My child is blind and cannot easily use a prepared text.

A. I suggest you contact NATHHAN (NATional cHallenged Homeschoolers Associated Network).* These wonderful people help families with children with special needs. They have become the main clearinghouse in the homeschool movement for information of this kind. Also contact the Library of Congress. They supply free use of Braille and large print materials for anyone who is legally blind. Your own state, also, should have resources.

*NATHHAN, 5383 Alpine Road SE, Olalla WA 98359. Phone 206-857-4257, FAX 206-857-7764, E-Mail: NATHANEWS@aol.com

Q. I have a friend who has a Down syndrome child. She has heard from other homeschoolers about nutritional supplements greatly helping their children's health and even learning ability. Do you know anything about these nutritional supplements, or where I can get more information?

A. From medical letters, I read that Down syndrome (sometimes written Down's Syndrome) children have an extra chromosome of number 21. Instead of the normal two, they have three. This was first discovered by Dr. Henry Turkel in the 1940s. Dr. Turkel had diagnosed Down syndrome as a disease of metabolism, so he treated it with antioxidant vitamins and other supplements. As usually happens in such cases, the FDA and the National Institutes of Health would not listen to him and suppressed his information, limiting his practice to the state of Michigan.

This extra chromosome causes extra production of superoxide dismutase. Health food store customers will recognize this as SOD, which is sold as a supplement. But Down syndrome children have too much of this good thing. To counteract this excess, alternative doctors suggest large amounts of the antioxidant vitamins C, A, E and betacarotene; and minerals zinc and selenium. Homeschool writer and special education consultant, Dianne Craft, is keeping up with the research in this area and some books suggested by her are listed below.* Though I have no experience with this, the testimonials I have read sound so amazing that I think you families affected by this should read up on it for yourselves.

*Debbie's Note: I have a friend here in Florida who has a Down syndrome child so I asked her about this vitamin therapy. She became very excited and told me they had been giving her son a vitamin compound** for five months, and had seen some surprising improvements. Her observation was that* he just seemed to "brighten up" and become more attentive after starting the therapy. They had been struggling over the years with potty training (he is now 4) and have just within the last few weeks achieved success. This is amazing to her, and she is definitely rejoicing over the gains he has made recently.

While it is more costly than regular vitamins, she feels that the health benefits and any other benefits that can come from it are worth the effort. She and her husband read all the information they could get, and discussed it with their doctor. The doctor discouraged her, but after prayer, they decided to give it a try. They are very pleased with the results. She especially appreciated the fact that they began sending her a free newsletter after she had contacted them for information. The newsletter, called "Bridges," consists mostly of parent letters which were a real blessing to them.

*Turkel. H. "The Medical Treatment for Down's Syndrome," Ubiotica, 19145 West Nine Mile Road, Southfield MI 40875. Copies available from Dr. Bernard Rimland, Autism Research Institute, 4182 Adams Avenue, San Diego CA 92116.

*Hoffer, A.M, and M. Walker, *Smart Nutrients,* Avery Publishing Group, NY.

*Dianne Craft can be contacted at 9150 Madre Place, Littleton CO 80124. Appointments for phone consultation can be made at 303-790-7458. At this writing the cost is $30 per half hour.

**Nutri-Chem, 1303 Richmond Road, Ottawa, Ontario, Canada K2B 7Y4. Phone: 613-820-9065 EST. (MSB Plus, Version 5 for Down syndrome children).

INDEX

About the Author

Dr. Ruth Beechick is mother of two and grandmother of four. Her sons grew up before the days of the modern homeschool movement, but as a lifelong educator she sees homeschooling as the healthiest movement in education today.

She received a bachelor's degree in music from Seattle Pacific University and, later, a master's and a doctorate in teaching and curriculum from Arizona State University. She spent a number of years in teaching and curriculum work in the public schools and college education departments, then spent a second career as editor and writer of Christian education materials. Now she continues writing from her home in the Rocky Mountains in Colorado.

More Books by this Author

The Three R's: Grades K-3. Three manuals for homeschooling parents explaining how and what to teach in reading, writing and arithmetic during the primary years.

You CAN Teach Your Child Successfully: Grades 4-8. Classic starter and reference book for homeschooling parents explaining how and what to teach in all subjects in the elementary grades.

The Language Wars: and Other Writings for Homeschoolers. A collection of twenty-five articles on education, including topics of history, Bible, phonics and language debates, dyslexia, testing, creativity, higher thinking, math, music, early childhood, and others.

A Biblical Psychology of Learning. Explains the error of modern psychologies, and how a biblical psychology leads to better education. Used by homeschoolers and in Christian colleges.

Language and Thinking for Young Children. Co-authored with Jeannie Nelson. Oral language activities especially for children who are not reading yet. Ages 5 to 7.

GENESIS: Finding Our Roots. Unique study integrating history, literature, art and other humanities with the first eleven chapters of Genesis.

Adam and His Kin: The Lost History of Their Lives and Times. Eye-opening view of Genesis 1—11 told as a narrative. Good read-aloud for homeschoolers.

The Cabin and the Ice Palace. Allegorical fiction with message of heaven and of creationism. Age 11 and up.

Christian Education Series

For teachers in Sunday school or other church programs. Also used by homeschoolers.

Teaching Preschoolers. Ages 2 and 3.
Teaching Kindergarteners. Ages 4 and 5.
Teaching Primaries. Grades 1 through 3.
Teaching Juniors. Grades 4 through 6.

About the Editor

Debbie Strayer is a native of Florida and received her bachelor's and master's degrees from Florida State University, where, also, she met Greg who became her husband. They have two children, young teenagers at the time of this book. The family can often be found at a baseball game watching Nathan play, or at a pool watching Ashley practice with her synchronized swimming team. They have been homeschooling for ten years.

In the public schools, Debbie served as a second grade teacher, a special education teacher, and assistant administrator of a remedial math and reading program. She now serves homeschoolers by giving the certified evaluations required by Florida law. She was editor of "Homeschooling Today"™ magazine for six years, and author of a column that brought encouragement to homeschoolers. She is a frequent conference and seminar speaker and is known for her humorous approach to the day-to-day events of life and for the practical help she can give to parents.

More Books by this Author

Gaining Confidence to Teach. Encourages homeschoolers practically and spiritually. The author's homeschool and professional education experience combine to provide support to all homeschoolers, from beginner to veteran.

Learning Language Arts through Literature

A graded series co-authored with Susan Simpson, integrating all the language arts and based on selections from good literature.

The Blue Book. A beginning reading program combining solid instruction with games, puppets and real books. Grades K-1.

The Red Book. Using the same approach of combining fun with skill learning, this text makes it easy for the homeschooling parent. Grade 2.

The Yellow Book. Takes topics of interest to young children and provides helpful and enjoyable practice of language arts skills, both new and old. Grade 3.

The Orange Book. Combines dictation lessons with topical studies such as newspapers, poetry, research, and making your own book. Grade 4.

The Purple Book. Teaches language skills using marvelous literature such as *Strawberry Girl* and *The Trumpet of the Swan* as its base. Grade 5.